W9-CJJ-040

BARE SOULS

BY

GAMALIEL BRADFORD

*Author of "The Soul of Samuel Pepys," "Damaged
Souls," "American Portraits," Etc.*

WITH ILLUSTRATIONS

NEW YORK AND LONDON
HARPER & BROTHERS
PUBLISHERS

883

920

BARE SOULS

First Edition

H–Y

TO

BETTY HEISER

WHOSE GRANDMOTHER READ MY SOUL BARE
AND WHOSE PRANKS AND FROLICS
DISTRACTED ME FROM
BARE SOULS

CONTENTS

LIST OF ILLUSTRATIONS

PREFACE

"The Soul of Samuel Pepys" and "Bare Souls" represent a digression from the extensive series of American portraits to which I mean in future to devote all my time and energy. I turned aside from this task partly because limitations of health made it difficult to carry on the necessary research, but mainly because the material for the American work is often scanty and inadequate, and I was curious to apply the psychographic method to the richest and most suggestive human documents that could be found. The "Diary of Pepys" and the correspondence of the various letter-writers studied in "Bare Souls" assuredly furnish such documents.

It will be noted that all the subjects portrayed in this volume were men of letters, all produced literary work of more or less importance. This by no means proves that all the great letter-writers have been authors, any more than it proves that all great authors have the genius for writing letters. But, other things being equal, the habit of facility with the pen gives letter-writing an added fluency and effectiveness. Moreover, the letters of distinguished persons, especially authors, are more likely to be preserved than those of less noted correspondents, though it is worth while to insist upon the fact, very obvious in most of the following portraits, that the letters which are preserved are apt to belong chiefly to later years.

The abnormal elements of the literary life are more or less evident in all the characters here studied. There is, for instance, the tendency to perpetual analysis: not only of others, not only of life in general, but even, perhaps especially, of the workings of the writer's own heart. Such analysis, when carried to excess, always tends to interfere with the play of natural instincts and impulses, to give a certain air of unreality and artificiality to the simplest and intensest habits and passions of our lives. Again, in all these literary men the desire for success—if not for wide renown, at least for intelligent recognition—plays so large a part that the recurrence of it might appear monotonous if it were not manifested in such different ways and with such varying richness of illustration and comment.

Another abnormal element, which did not strike me until I had made my selection and partly worked it out, is that only one of all these eight letter-writers was married, and that one, Fitzgerald, took a wife only as it were by accident and hardly kept her long enough for her to become a serious consideration in his spiritual development. The negative results of this curious common lack would be too complicated and too varied to follow out; but it is clear that eight lives so cut off from the more normal conditions of human existence in a domestic establishment with wife and children, must naturally present many features, both practical and spiritual, which would be quite out of the regular course.

Yet, in spite of such undeniably erratic and unusual manifestations, the impression of common humanity in all these great letter-writers must, I think, far outweigh any sense of eccentricity or exception. In the intense vitality of Voltaire, in the shy seclusion of Gray, in the timid obsessions of Cowper, in the frolic, all-dissolving merriment of Lamb, in the eager and passionate indolence of Fitzgerald, we must all surely find traces and touches of our own hearts. And these splendid masters of words have used them mainly to lay bare the inmost secrets not of their own souls only, but of yours and mine and everyone's.

GAMALIEL BRADFORD

Wellesley Hills, Massachusetts.

I
A CLUE TO THE LABYRINTH OF SOULS

All at once the surface of life is torn apart, and we read bare soul.

SAINTE-BEUVE.

BARE SOULS

A CLUE TO THE LABYRINTH OF SOULS

ONE of the best known quotations from Sainte-Beuve is that in which he describes his literary specialty: "I botanize, I herborize, I am a naturalist of souls." Assuredly there is no branch of the naturalist's work which is more fascinating than this—and more uncertain and deceptive. The student of birds and flowers and insects deals in the main with classes; every sparrow is a sparrow. But the naturalist of souls deals with individual human beings, all astonishingly, perplexingly, delightfully different. There is no end to the richness and variety of the material. Sometimes even it is difficult to find the beginning of it.

How to get at souls: the inner, hidden, mysterious machinery so cunningly and completely masked behind the solid, compact covering of flesh and blood? How to penetrate this covering, to dissect it, to seize and grasp and analyze the strange

3

web of passions and emotions and experiences that lies beneath? The mere outer covering, taken in itself, taken statically as it were, tells us so little. There are people who pretend to read souls from faces. Alas, it sometimes seems as if the more they pretended the less they knew.

> "There's no art
> To find the mind's construction in the face,"

says the great master, who perhaps found as much as any one. The cast of the features, the set of eyes and nose and mouth and chin, tell us something, but how vaguely, and how differently according to the different observer.

When men and women begin to act and to speak, the clues become more abundant. The soul will shine out in the smile, in the intonation, in the gesture, even little trifling ones. If you know what to look for, minor, insignificant actions tell you much, perhaps more than greater, more deliberate deeds, because there is less thought or care for concealment. Yet, even so, the problem of interpretation is infinitely complicated. Behind the act is a motive, some motive, it may be many motives; but to distinguish and disentangle these is

4

a task to make the boldest hesitate to say, with the
soothsayer in "Antony and Cleopatra,"

> "In nature's infinite book of secrecy
> A little I can read."

Moreover, the historian and biographer is not
often able to study the action and speech of his subjects directly. He has to take the reports of others.
And these reports are unreliable and conflicting to
an almost incredible degree. Until one has worked
long on such things, one finds it hard to understand
how thoughtful, fair-minded observers can differ so
completely in their record of men's lives. And all
observers are not fair-minded, or even thoughtful.
Therefore, at the very outset the biographer finds
a veil drawn between him and the soul he is attempting to study, a veil all the more confusing
and ensnaring and smothering when its surface is
deceitfully radiant and transparent.

When we come to what a man has actually written himself, actually set down as the record of his
own thoughts in black and white, we find the clues
to soul more abundant, if not always more reliable.
If we can eliminate intentional deception on the
writer's part as, alas, we cannot always, and if we
are competent to weigh and measure, and, as it

were, dissect his language and expressions, we may be able to travel the road traced by his pen into the shadowy regions of his spirit. But words are not always fruitful in this regard, and the very abundance of them is apt to be misleading, discouraging, and wearisome. An author's complete works may fill a dozen or a score of volumes. You think, surely a man cannot have written all this without telling me all about his soul that I want to know. Alas, you plunge in and turn page after page, and the result is too often—plain nothing. Charles Sumner's speeches fill twelve volumes. They were very good speeches and no doubt answered their purpose. But the soul of Charles Sumner—is not there or is there only in very vague and elusive bits and snatches. Cicero had far more soul than Sumner, and far more gift of revealing it; yet from his speeches alone you can get much less than you would wish.

But men write other things than speeches, and some men have kindly described for us their own souls. There are clues enough here, of course; yet even here the clues are less numerous than one might desire, and especially they are less trustworthy. Formal autobiographies are generally written in old age. At that period, the memories

6

of the earlier part of life, the more important, constructive part, are apt to be distorted and confused, to be altered and twisted out of normal proportions and relations in a way that would astonish even the writers, if they could test their recollection by the actual record of facts. Autobiography is a fascinating form of literature, but it is a terribly deceptive one, unless it can be checked by other testimony of a very different character.

The daily diary is better, and our richest clues to the great field of souls are probably arrived at in this way. There are the directly personal diaries, in which skilled and scientific analysts have endeavored to set down the daily process of their lives with the most minute and anxious care. Yet, with all their care and all their anxiety, it is astonishing how often the diligent and impartial observer from the outside feels that they have been mistaken. Long ago an old Greek poet said, "many things are obscure to man, but nothing is more obscure to him than his own soul." One feels this in reading the Journal of Amiel, or that of Maine de Biran. Subtle and penetrating as the writers are, they seem to be struggling with a problem beyond their reach or that of any one. The very fact of so constantly observing one's own life tends to make the living of it artificial and distorted and it sometimes appears that the more objective diarists, such as Greville or Moore or Pepys, give a truer rendering, even of their inner lives, than the deliberate analyst.

But, after all, only a portion of mankind keeps diaries, and the process is in itself rather artificial. Practically all men and women who can write at all write letters, and letters afford, on the whole, the most general and the most satisfactory clues for the naturalist of souls. Letter writing in some form goes back to the earliest written records that we have, though its spiritually interpretative value can hardly be said to begin before the ages of more highly developed civilization. It is sometimes urged that in the present day the art of letter writing is dying out. Certainly the hurry of modern life does not favor long letters. Also, who would write when he can use the telephone? And the growing habit of dictation and stenography is maddeningly destructive to the old personality and significance of the exquisite epistolary art. Yet, so long as men burn to pour out their souls to each other, and so long as there are people—and there are millions of them—who can say with the pen what they cannot say with the tongue, so long will letters be written: significant letters, human letters,

8

letters whose stinging, darting, quivering phrases afford an intentional or unintentional clue to the writers' souls. An age which has seen within one year the publication of the letters of Walter Page, James Huneker, and H. H. Furness need not feel that the art of letter writing is dying out.

It would be a pity if it did; for, quite independent of their psychographical value, letters have a singular charm for those who have learned to savor them. And this is not a matter of general literary genius. To be sure some great authors, like Cicero and Voltaire, have been great letter writers also. But the most delightful of letter writers have often not been authors in other lines at all. Madame de Sévigné, for instance, is universally recognized as a mistress of the epistolary art. She wrote nothing else whatever. So with Madame du Deffand. So with men. There is the French letter writer, Doudan, one of the most varied and brilliant, who has no reputation as a general author. There is our own Francis J. Child, whose letters were published a few years ago, a great scholar, who might perhaps have written more generally, if he had wished, but at any rate an exquisite letter writer, and one who should be more widely known. On the other hand, Sainte-Beuve and Matthew Arnold.

9

both poets and critics of the greatest distinction and both masters in the use and interpretation of the letters of others, themselves wrote letters that were dull, tame, and insignificant.

As to the substance of letters, there is the external and the internal, what affects others, and what affects the writer himself. Externally, there is the larger treatment of life, the picture of historical periods and characters. From this point of view letters are often historical documents of the highest consequence and value. There are such accumulations as the Paston Letters which, in giving the minute portrayal of the daily life of an average family, afford at the same time a priceless record of the manners of a whole period. There are the letters of distinguished historical personages, shedding floods of light on the great events and actions of their time; for example, the vast correspondence of Thomas Jefferson, said to be the most extensive known and to run to twenty thousand letters, of which eight or ten thousand are actually in print. Also, private individuals who note and study what is going on about them may render the life of their age with a color and a human suggestiveness that can be conveyed by no formal history. The large collection of Horace

10

Walpole's letters is one of the monuments of both English history and literature. And the even larger collection of Voltaire's is more significant still. In fact, when you take Voltaire's own letters in connection with what are addressed to him— letters from Frederick the Great, from Catherine Second, from D'Alembert, from Rousseau, from Diderot, from Madame du Deffand, from Madame d'Epinay—you have probably the greatest epistolary treasure the world has ever seen or will see. It is the epitome of the French, and indeed of the general, eighteenth century.

Nor are letters important only in the larger portrayal of historical periods and movements. They are full of information about human life and character in all lines. A keen observer, one who is naturally and instinctively interested in the workings of motive and passion, will note and jot down in intimate correspondence the most exquisitely suggestive details of the dramas that are constantly playing about him. This is especially true of women letter writers. They are not always fertile in abstract discussion of great problems; but they are inexhaustible in watching and catching those little bits of emotion and experience that tell us more about souls than the pompous and academic

11

reasoning of pretentious philosophy. How quick and varied and spirited is Madame de Sévigné's rendering of life! What unforgettable pictures does she draw of the people about her and their doings and sufferings! And Lady Mary Montagu —whether she is describing what happens in Turkey or what happens in London, there is the same intense, vivid touch that makes you see and feel as she does.

It is in the play of these light, casual, informal renderings that the humor of the letter writer shows its greatest fascination. What a comedy will Charles Lamb make of a dull evening at cards, or the tedious call of an uninvited and unanticipated visitor! Or again, Cowper, when he forgets to be obsessed by eternal damnation, will draw the liveliest and most amusing sketch of things and people which another would find perfectly commonplace and insignificant.

But the naturalist of souls is more particularly concerned with letters as revealing the character of the writer. Here the first distinction to make is between the conscious, literary letter and that which springs genuinely from the heart. To be sure, it is not always easy to draw an arbitrary line. One can never be quite confident that the writer of a letter has not some sort of publicity in mind, and with distinguished authors such a consciousness is almost inevitable. But one can recognize and put aside at once the letters of extreme artificiality, like those of James Howell and the earlier Balzac, clever enough in their way often and historically valuable, but evidently composed with the printer in mind. For the psychographer and naturalist such letters have little value. And at the other extreme we have letters like those of Fitzgerald or Doudan, clearly written in the most private intimacy of friendship, without the faintest thought of a larger audience than the eye or ear to which they are addressed. These are usually the letters of greatest charm, and they are always those that give most information to the analyst of souls.

Even in letters that are manifestly sincere, however, there is an astonishing difference in the element of self-revelation. Some writers, with the best will in the world, cannot seem to give themselves: they are formal, external, perfunctory, perhaps tell a good deal about others, but are shy and retiring as to their own lives. I found an interesting illustration of this in the letters of General Lee. There are many of these, but they tell us surprisingly little. And the fascination of studying such

13

a subject is rather enhanced by the difficulty. Certainly there is a singular charm about running across startling and illuminating touches of human truth, as one is almost sure to in the end.

Then there are spirits of an opposite order, spirits whose own life and experience seem to flow naturally into their letters, and who give you on every page the subtlest and profoundest insight into the secrets of their lives. Take Horace Walpole and Voltaire. Walpole is always posing. He sometimes reveals his heart, but he does it against his will. Voltaire, for all he was in actual life too often an expert and unscrupulous liar, is the most sincere and self-revealing of letter writers. His whole soul flares out at you every moment in sparkling, glowing, sputtering, infectious vitality. Nor is it only the egotists who open their hearts. Fitzgerald and Child were the simplest, shyest of men; yet their letters are a mine for the naturalist of souls. Every human experience is reflected in such letters, touched often lightly and swiftly, with implication rather than development, but all the more telling in the intense impression of bare truth. Every passion that stirs and agitates the frail substance of mortality thrills and quivers in the slight or solid missives which these busy thinkers

14

and feelers toss back and forth to each other.
Love? Love has been a mainstay of letters since
they were first written. Normal love is there, if
love is ever normal, and the old story constantly re-
news its freshness, till one is reminded of the pretty
saying of the French comedy, "Behold another
lover who thinks she has invented love." And there
is love abnormal, all its disappointment, love in
quaint, remote developments, like Madame du
Deffand's septuagenarian ardor for Horace Walpole, or the self-tormenting ecstasy with which
Madame de Sévigné enveloped her pedantic
daughter.

Hate? It naturally finds less place in letters, because one pours out one's life to those one loves, but
hardly to those one hates. Yet Dr. Johnson loved
a good hater, and there are plenty of them in the
epistolary world. Fierce and eager souls, like
Swift's or Voltaire's, lash their enemies with a vigor
and splendor of language perhaps even more effec-
tive than that which they lavish on admiration or
tenderness. "He who does not know how to hate
does not know how to love," says Voltaire.

And there is money, which plays such a large and
vital part in all the practical concerns of life. The
zeal for it, the lack of it, the delight in getting it,

15

the luxury of spending it—all are everywhere reflected in men's and women's letters. Take the pregnant, profound, bitter observation of Gray in regard to it: "It is a foolish thing, that one can't only not live as one pleases, but where and with whom one pleases, without money. Swift somewhere says, that money is liberty; and I fear money is friendship too and society, and almost every external blessing. It is a great though ill-natured comfort to see most of those who have it in plenty, without pleasure, without liberty, and without friends."

The workings of ambition, of the passion for glory, are constantly unveiled and betrayed in the great letter writers: so many of them were authors or artists or statesmen, successful or disappointed. But it is pretty to see how often the passion is dissembled, how reluctantly acknowledged. Glory? Oh, no, I am not working for glory; for this, that, or the other, but not for glory: glory is not worth while. And yet day and night the reward is in their thoughts. Sometimes one meets the admission of it in remote, unexpected corners, as in the remark of Cowper: "I have (what, perhaps, you little suspect me of) in my nature an infinite share of ambition." How few men or women who are worth anything have not?

And ambition prompts and requires labor. Many of the great workers of the world have written letters, and into them casually flows the suggestion of vast, unremitting toil. Work is not only the vulgar means of support, it is the agent of distinction, the surest and sanest remedy for pain and sorrow, the one firm, unfailing comfort in a world of profitless reflection and burdensome leisure. Watch the torment, the enthusiasm, the exhaustion, the splendid stimulus of work in the letters of Voltaire, or in those of Flaubert. All its terrors, all its secrets, and all its triumphs are revealed there.

If you have not the zest or the gift or, perhaps, the physical ability for work, there opens and yawns beside you inevitably the dead, blank gulf of ennui, or boredom, and all the flowers of diversion that you seek to strew over it will not hide it entirely. This insidious, rotting malady of ennui creeps into many lovely letters, but nowhere is it more subtly dissected than in the correspondence of Madame du Deffand. She analyzes it, she battles with it, she strives to keep it out of her communication with her friends; but still it crushes her and blights and strangles life: "I know that one augments one's ills by telling them to one's friends: you pour your ennui upon them, and ennui is the tomb of every tender feeling."

Also, there is more positive misery than ennui; there is the subtle, pervading melancholy which comes from brooding too widely and too deeply upon the hidden mysteries of life. Strangely enough, when one is afflicted with this malady the reading of the words of others who have known it is rather a consolation than an added grief. It has been shrewdly suggested that all the great letter writers are more or less melancholy. But this is hardly exact. Madame de Sévigné had the gayest, sweetest, brightest of spirits. Voltaire was certainly not melancholy, except as he was everything by turns. But it is true that extensive letter writing is generally done by thoughtful and observant persons. And in this mixed world in which we are condemned to live and die, thought and observation are great breeders of sadness. Even the most humorous of letter writers, like Lamb and Cowper and Heine, seem sometimes to use humor as a mask for care and grief too deep for common utterance, and if you probe the jest you are apt to find the tear beneath it. At any rate, in writers like Flaubert and Gray the sombre depths

18

of life are revealed with an intensity of anguish that is as tragic as it is human.

And then those who feel grief most are naturally most zealous in seeking the various refuges that are afforded from it, and all the varied multiplicity of these is amply displayed in the pages of the masters of letter writing. There is beauty. Take painting and music as we find them suggested in Fitzgerald —always with restraint, always with delicacy, but with passionate appreciation, nevertheless. Take the splendor of poetry and literature generally, as we find it in Keats and Flaubert. And nature— the vast, soothing, unfailing consolation of nature is developed in the great letters of the world perhaps more exquisitely than anywhere but in the greatest poetry. Does not even Voltaire murmur: "The streams, the flowers, and the woods console, too often men do not."

Another refuge from melancholy is thought. Thought is the cause of it, and thought is often the very best cure. We do not look for elaborate, developed philosophy in letters, or if we do we seldom find it. But these rich, highly-cultivated, widely-nourished spirits take the great problems of the world and play with them, toss them about sometimes lightly and casually, as a kitten does a ball of thread, and in doing it they strike out thoughts which we can carry away with us and live on for days and days.

And perhaps the best of all these refuges is God, and again the letter writers—without being, most of them, professedly religious—have most precious revelations to make to us, if not as to the nature of God himself, at least as to the breadth and depth of His relation to humanity and His strange, infinite importance to it. God is not only predominant in the morbid musings of Cowper; He touches the wide, worldly contemplation of Cicero, He hovers over the sparkling pages of Madame de Sévigné, He is not wholly absent from the sceptical mocking of Voltaire, He intrudes dimly into the remote solitude of Gray, and suggests His presence in the delicate shy reserve of Fitzgerald. He is literally everywhere in the intimate communings of Eugénie de Guérin. In the curious, mad burst of genius which came from our own Emily Dickinson the sense of God is so overpowering that the reader is almost swept away into the unearthly atmosphere in which the writer lived: no room for ennui or melancholy there.

Even yet we have barely touched this vast field of letters, so inexhaustible in its fascination and charm. Through these manifold, twinkling, sparkling pages something of the past beckons us, whispers us, instructs us, perplexes us, delights us, and, above all, in the magic phrase of Keats, "teazes us out of thought as doth eternity."

II
VOLTAIRE

CHRONOLOGY

François Marie Arouet de Voltaire.

Born, 1694.

In Bastille, falsely accused of satirical verse, 1716.

In Bastille, after quarrel with Duc de Sully, 1725.

In England, 1726-1729.

Lived with Madame du Châtelet, mainly at Cirey, 1733-1749.

In Berlin, 1750-1753.

Lived near Geneva, 1754-1778.

Bought Ferney, 1758.

Died, May 30, 1778, in Paris.

VOLTAIRE

I

FRANÇOIS AROUET, better known by the literary
name which he preferred, Voltaire, is most familiar
to us as he appeared in age: the lean, wrinkled,
withered face; the vivid, mocking eye, which seemed
to see the underside of everything, the figure
shrunken and shattered by the fierce, restless intelligence, which soared and plunged and darted
into the deepest hiding-places of human folly and
vanity and wickedness. It was the incomparable
vigor of this devouring intellect that made Voltaire
the greatest spiritual influence of the mid-eight-
eenth century, and one of the greatest of the
world. The influence of Rousseau upon posterity
may be more picturesque, more flamboyant, more
melodramatic; but Voltaire's was probably more
subtly diffused and more fundamentally stimulating. Moreover, we must remember Rousseau's
debt to Voltaire.

As to the quality of Voltaire's influence there will always be dispute, so long as men look at life from different angles. The conservative, the orthodox, those who think that sacred things—or even things that appear sacred—should never be touched will regard him with loathing and horror. He sapped, they say, the necessary conventions and respectabilities of life, and took pleasure in such sapping. Decency was unknown to him. With the evil, dirty mischief of a satyr he skipped through sanctities and decorums, tearing off and snatching away, giggling and gurgling with hateful and corrupting laughter. He sapped religion, made God a jest, and the dearest things of God, turned the sweet, quiet devotion of pure souls into foul and turbulent mocking, tipped over the large and painfully erected fabric of the Christian universe and danced upon the ruins as if it were a gay thing to leave mankind neither pity nor piety nor love nor hope.

He was a destroyer by his own confession, say these excellent conservatives, *"Je suis grand démolisseur,"* [1] and what place has a struggling, battling, laboriously constructing world for destroyers? When they are destroyers of genius they are all the more damnable. Voltaire was a mere

negative, a minus quantity, with a terrible force of
infection, which dragged thousands of high and fine
souls, who might have been constructive, over to
the negative side.

To which Voltaire's admirers reply that in a
sense it is all true enough. He was a destroyer,
and past question he enjoyed it. All children like
to destroy, and in many aspects Voltaire was singularly a child. But what did he destroy? He was
born into a rotten social world. The poor were
downtrodden, crushed, embittered. The rich were
cynical, self-indulgent, careless. A huge frame-
work of artificial convention sustained the aristocratic structure of French, of European society.
Kings and all their paraphernalia were outworn,
useless, burdensome. Yet they persisted, with
more tyrannous iniquity, the more they found their
power failing. Voltaire sailed right into all these
things, not with dynamite, which would have
brought him to the scaffold, not with slow theorizing, which would have brought him nowhere, but
with subtle irony and mocking, which showed the
vanity of pretence and the folly of convention,
without giving direct excuse for cutting off his
head to get him out of the way.

So with religion; what Voltaire attacked, or

meant to attack, was the narrowness of it, the cruelty of it, the distortion of it in the hands of meddlesome, encroaching, ignorant priests and superstitious, groveling laymen. In his general tumbling-over of idols no doubt some good things and good people got hard knocks, and justly resented it. It must always be so. But the temple had grown dusty and sombre, webbed all over with spiders and befouled with bats and other ugly creatures who make their abode in darkness. Voltaire smashed the glooming windows, threw wide the leather-shrouded doors, and let in light and air and the broad serenity and sanity of heaven. Are these things nothing? Is liberty negative? Is truth negative, even when she comes in her austerest garb, wielding the fierce scourge with which she scatters lies? "My aim is to diminish, if possible, the weight of evil which overloads and devours this globe of misery." [2] Is that the cry of a man who labored only to destroy?

Voltaire's claims to positive and permanent recognition have never been better stated than by Sainte-Beuve, who, nevertheless, was anything but a Voltairian and did not hesitate to point out repeatedly the great man's extraordinary defects and pettiness: "Voltaire was sincere, passionate, pos-

VOLTAIRE

sessed till his latest breath by the desire to change, to ameliorate, to perfect the world about him. He was a missionary of common sense. Until his last hour and as long as his intellect remained alive, he repelled with horror what seemed to him dishonest and false. In his noble, perpetual fever he was one of those who have the right to say: *Est deus in nobis.* So long as his heart beat, he had in him what I call the good demon, a sacred indignation and ardor. Apostle of reason to the very end, it may be said of Voltaire that he died fighting." [3]

And Victor Hugo sums it up in one of his clever lines,

"Voltaire, grand homme, et peu Voltairien." [4]

II

In any case there is one thing about Voltaire that his bitterest enemy cannot dispute and that his friends rejoice in—his enormous vitality. From infancy to age every particle of him seemed to live, to vibrate and quiver with an intense, inexhaustible, irrepressible animation, which entered into all his thoughts and deeds and extended itself to every thing and person that came near him. He sums it up in three words: *"J'aime tout,"* "I like everything." [5] The things he did not like he hated, and he often liked and hated the same thing, as the mood took him. He might be angry, he might be discouraged, he might be weary, he might be desperate: he was never indolent and never indifferent. Life was a great game or, if you preferred, a great battle; but while you lived you must make the most of it, must make every nerve and muscle you had tell something and do something. If you did not, where was the use of your living? "I have got to fight, yet I am ill unto death; so there you have my history." [6]

For it must be observed at the start that Voltaire's superb spiritual vigor did not mean physical vigor at all. On the contrary, his life seems to have been a constant struggle with ill health, at any rate the portion of it that is fully recorded for us. All the more notable is it that no ill health could crush him. "I carry an enormous burden, and it charms me." [7] That is the tone. He liked struggling with difficulties, external or internal; it made him feel that he was alive every minute. Yet the history of his physical ills is exhibited to us with minute detail and constant repetition. In any one else it would be tedious, but nothing can be tedious in him. He envies good health, thinks what could be done with it, and what could be enjoyed, though one wonders how he could have done more or enjoyed more, whatever health he had. His best wish for a friend is that he may keep his taste for good victuals: "I am sorry for poor brother Menou; but I hope that he will not lose his appetite. He was born hungry and gay: that birthright ought to console for everything." [8] As for himself, appetite fails, eyesight fails, hearing fails, the stomach is wrong, the liver is wrong, the heart is wrong. He has plenty to complain of in youth: "I suffer three quarters of the day, and the other quarter I do very little work." [9] And it would hardly be expected that the complaint would diminish in age: "I am a little deaf, a little blind, a little impotent; and on top of this are two or three abominable special infirmities; but nothing destroys my hope." [10] Nothing could destroy it. Or rather, it was not so much hope as the tremendous ardor of living, which nothing could extinguish but actual death.

Nor did the ill-health keep him still, force him to a sedentary, secluded, self-cherishing existence. Much the contrary. "Nothing is more wholesome than to keep going," he cries.[11] He kept going, with his limbs when he could, with his spirit always.

From his birth in 1694 to his death in 1778 he gives the impression of being perpetually a creature of motion, and for the imperfect means of movement in those days, his actual locomotion was wonderful. He skipped about France, he wandered into England, he sojourned in Prussia, he established various abiding places in Switzerland. It is true that he could say exquisite things about peace and quiet and home. He could say exquisite things about anything—and at the moment mean them. "After you have sought over the wide world, you learn that happiness is to be found only in your own home." [12] And in his later years he did cling quite closely to his lovely retreat at Ferney, in the neighborhood of Geneva, where he could jump at a moment's notice from one country to another if either government got too troublesome. Yet it was the movement and excitement and triumph of a final trip to Paris that hastened his death. And always the excitement of such trips was deliciously exhilarating to him. With what mad fervor does he protest against the distraction of them, and how he enjoys it. "I go. I come. I sup at one end of the town, to sup the next night at the other. From a company of three or four intimate friends you have to fly to the Opera, to the Comedy, have to

see the curiosities like any stranger, to embrace a
hundred persons in one day, make and accept a
hundred protestations: not one instant to yourself,
no time to write, or think, or sleep. I am like the
old Roman who was smothered under the flowers
that were heaped upon him." [13] To the last gasp
he liked the flowers and all that went with them.

Voltaire's intense vitality in the practical affairs
of men is written on every page of his correspondence. Money? He has plenty to say about
money, and deals with it as a gross daily necessity
which everybody ought to recognize as such. He
was not born with any particular abundance of it
—in fact had a very moderate purse, such as suited
his moderate station—but with the tastes of a mil-
lionaire. Yet he appreciates that the lack of material resources may be a wholesome spur to doing
great things in the world. As if he needed any!
"There is a difference so immense between a man
who has his fortune all made and one who has it to
make that they are not creatures of the same
species." [14] To the end of his life he retained
those curious streaks of petty parsimony which are
apt to appear in persons who have suffered from
financial pressure in their younger days. He would
haggle and chaffer over the details of a bargain,

and cheat, if necessary. For all his undeniable love of abstract truth, his vivid imagination constantly led him into misrepresentations which might be called plain lies, and really were so. The whole of his wretched transaction with the President de Brosses over a land bargain is disreputable, and Brosses had every reason for calling him "a man admirable, indeed, for his talents, but in business matters turbulent, unjust, and tricky, without really understanding them"; [15] and for summing up his character, "in spite of your weaknesses, you will always be a great man—in your writings." [16] Yet with all the apparent meanness and greed, which it is impossible to explain away, Voltaire could be splendidly liberal and generous, could squander money on great causes and poor people, could spend like a prince and live like one, as well as write and think like a genius.

He enjoyed the comfort and luxury that money brought, enjoyed the display of it, doing things on a grand scale and having others feel that he did so. When he got a country estate of his own, he liked to ornament and develop it and make it worthy of the greatest writer of the age. He liked to have a lot of dependents and hangers-on, men working with him and for him, to control them and have them feel that he did: "I love passionately to be master in my own house." [17] He was a builder, was always busy with some new structure for use or ornament: "If you meet pious people, tell them that I have finished my church, and that the Pope, has sent me relics for it; if you meet pleasant people, tell them that I have finished my theatre." [18] It delighted him to pose as an industrious, respectable, and innocent country gentleman: "I get in my harvests, I plant, I build, I am establishing a colony, perhaps for somebody to destroy: these are very serious occupations." [19]

But it is evident that what above all interested him was humanity. Whether he was building, or buying, or writing, or lying, he was an intensely human creature, and everything human was akin to him. He was interested in the world at large. Princes attracted him, and peasants also. Soldiers were impressive, priests were exasperating, scholars were instructive, fools were amusing, and generally men and women were wonderful always, as well in their glory as in their every-day pettiness. His immense correspondence brought him gossip and scandal, as well as solid historical information, from all over the world, and he reveled in both. England, Holland, Germany, Russia, Turkey, Italy,

and Spain—all were delightful stamping grounds
for his riotous imagination. He loved men for the
best of possible reasons—because they were in all
essential respects what he was: "Whoever has
imagination and insight can find in himself the full
knowledge of human nature; for all men are alike
at bottom, and the difference of shades does not
alter the fundamental color." [20]

And if he liked to read and hear about men at
a distance, he liked to meet them personally. He
sometimes insisted that he did not, but he did. In
his retirement at Ferney he always had swarms of
people about him, entertained them at his table,
read poems to them, acted plays to them, flattered
them, scolded them, complained that they inter-
fered with his work and then worked more than any
other three.

As to women, Voltaire was of course vastly
acquainted with them, as with men—chatted with
them, corresponded with them, accepted their adulation with delight. Love was different. It was
excellent stuff to make literature of, too often
literature not very decent. For life it was decoying
but dangerous. No doubt there were adventures
in his youth. Some of his early love letters exist;
but they are not particularly convincing. When he

WILLIAM COWPER

was twenty-four he announces: "I find it is ridiculous for me to be in love, and still more ridiculous for any one to love me. That settles it: I give it up for life." [21] He lived affectionately with Madame du Châtelet for a number of years and her death seems to have shaken him more than any other experience: "I have not lost a mistress, I have lost half of myself, a soul for which mine was made." [22] But in general it is clear that he was not born a lover: he was too immensely and vividly full of himself. It is most interesting to distinguish this warm, quick, superficial vitality, like a Leyden jar, always ready to snap and sparkle but never touched to the depths—because there were no depths—from a nature, like Catullus for example, all concentrated in one profound, devouring obsession of passion. You cannot imagine Voltaire's writing or feeling Catullus's fiery distich:

> "I love, I hate; but do not ask me why:
> I know it, and I feel it, and I die."

Of course Voltaire loved and hated both, and was quick and eager in both of them. *"I love* is a fine word," he says; "but you should not repeat it too often; sometimes you should say, I hate." [23] Only in both perhaps his expression was a little more furious than his real feeling. At any rate, the feeling did not go deep, or last long. But he did have an exuberance of quarrels, so much so that it sometimes seems as if his whole life was nothing but a succession of them. "This world is a perpetual war, prince with prince, priest with priest, people with people, scribbler with scribbler." [24] And he rather liked it, liked it very decidedly. The sword, indeed, was not his natural weapon. But his tongue and his pen were magnificent instruments and, alas, such instruments may be used more brilliantly to lash than even to flatter. He did lash, and scourge, and scarify; crack his stinging whip over great malefactors and petty vermin who were not worth it, sometimes with splendid courage, sometimes with small malevolence. Then, when it was over, he commonly forgot all about it. He could, to be sure, make fun of his own Christian spirit: "Really, I overlooked the article of forgiving injuries. The injuries most felt, they say, are railleries. I forgive with all my heart those whom I have mocked." [25] But he did not cherish persistent grudges, or indeed care enough about his enemies to harbor long vengeance. There were too many of them and it was too amusing to

38

make new ones. "This world is warfare: I love to
carry it on, it puts life into me." [26]

The most picturesque of all Voltaire's personal
ruptures, and one of the great quarrels of the world,
was his break with Frederick the Great. The study
of their relation, its growth and violent severance
and frigid renewal is a curious piece of psychological analysis. As a young crown prince with literary tastes, Frederick was fascinated by Voltaire's
genius, and the great French author was naturally
flattered by such princely admiration. They ex-
changed letter after letter, passing compliments,
witty sarcasms, and naughty stories, and Frederick
submitted his verses and Voltaire criticized them
with tact and patience and kindly suggestion.
Then Frederick's father died and the new king was
anxious to have the amusement and the glory of
Voltaire's presence at his court. For a long time
Voltaire held off, well divining the danger. But at
last he yielded and established himself in Berlin.
The result might easily have been foreseen, and
both ought to have foreseen it. But at first Voltaire was charmed. The king was all a king could
be—soldier, scholar, patron, friend. "It seems as
if nature had made him expressly for me: all my
hours are delicious. I have not discovered the least

thorn in my roses." [27]   Then the doubt, the dis-
comfort, the dissatisfaction creep in, oh, so subtly,
so delicately.   There is the superb "but" passage:
"My life is free and abundantly occupied; but, but
—operas, comedies, balls, suppers at Sans-Souci,
war-manœuvres, concerts, studies, lectures; but,
but—the city of Berlin, large, far better arranged
than Paris, palaces, theatres, kindly queens, charming princesses, lovely maids of honor . . . : but,
but—my dear child, the weather is beginning to
turn cold." [28]   It turned colder, and colder yet.
Whose the fault was it is not necessary to de-
termine, or rather it is quite evident that there was
a luxury of fault on both sides.   Given an arbitrary, cynical, satirical, selfish prince and an
equally arbitrary, satirical, susceptible author, disaster was clearly inevitable.   It came after three
years.   The only wonder is that it did not come
sooner.   The whole world was delighted with the
scandalous exhibition of great men's tempers.   Voltaire got away with considerable difficulty, and during a lengthy interval there were no more of those
amiable letters.   Later they were renewed, but they
were never quite the same.

It should, however, be remembered and appreciated that Voltaire's nature was warm and respon-

sive in his affections as in his quarrels. His family ties were not deeply binding, at least so far as we know them. He expressed a good deal of tenderness for his nieces, and one of them, Madame Denis, kept his house for a long time. But she does not seem to have been a very attaching person. Outside the domestic circle he had hosts of friends and to some of them he continued loyally devoted for many years. With his gift of expressing everything, he said delightful and satisfying words about friendship. "Little annoyances pass, friendship remains: that is why we should cherish life." [29]

Among these numerous friends of Voltaire's there were naturally many besides Frederick of a station in life much superior to his own, and he is often accused of flattering such outrageously. He had the art of saying nice things and liked to do so, and he knew well that the great as well as the little like to have nice things said to them. But he, and they, understood that it was a good deal a matter of saying. Underneath he had his self-respect, and knew how to maintain it, with Frederick as well as others. With friends nearer to his own rank he was charming in cordiality and no doubt sincere in tenderness. He did indeed have a keen sense of mutual obligation, and much of his correspondence consists of asking somebody to do something. But it is quite evident that he was ready to take his turn at doing, and his long-continued relations with Cideville, with Thieriot, with the D'Argentals show both respect and deep affection.

As to humanity in the larger, peculiarly eighteenth century sense, no one can dispute that Voltaire was richly endowed with it. He himself tells us so on all occasions, but there is plenty of indirect evidence that is perhaps more convincing. "The greatest privilege of a human being is to be able to do good." [30] It is somewhat general, but it is unquestionably sincere. As in so many other things, he anticipated his age in sympathy for animals: "The dumb creatures, our brethren, deserve a little more attention than we give them . . . I wish we might discover preventives for the contagious maladies of animals, when they are in health, so that we might apply them when they are diseased." [31] And his sympathy for the sufferings of men was far more intense. Wrong, injustice, cruelty irritated him—infuriated him—and he protested against them with all the ardor of his heart and his pen, his satire and his mockery: "I have discovered frightful things, infamous things, execrable things, which will make your hair stand

42

on end, if you have any hair." [32] Nor was the protest merely general. His efforts to assist the unfortunate in the cases of Calas, Sirven, and others cost him time, money, and friends, and he was ready to risk a great deal to see justice done. It is true that he was attacking the Jesuits and other things and people whom he hated, and this was agreeable in itself. Still, the result was positive and noble, and must be credited to him so long as humanity detests intolerance and loves the right.

III

The vitality which Voltaire poured out in all these external relations, is perhaps even more manifest in intellectual and spiritual matters. Everything he touched, he touched with ardor, and in the course of that long and varied life there were few things that he did not touch.

As with many writers, the fine arts outside of his own made comparatively little appeal to him. No doubt he felt the beauty of painting and sculpture, but the conditions were so different from those of literature that they seemed trammeling: "Sculpture and painting are, it seems to me, like music, they will not express the finer elements of what we call *esprit*. The cleverness of an epigram can never be rendered by a musician and a subtle allegory, which exists only for the intelligence, cannot be expressed by either painter or sculptor." [33] For music he seems to have had the indifference of other men of letters. "As for the music, it is said to be good. I know nothing about it: I have never been able to appreciate the remarkable merit of double crotchets . . . I have always compared French music to draughts and Italian music to checkers. It is something to have overcome difficulties." [34]

Nor was Voltaire much more susceptible to nature than to the charms of music. He liked to live in the country, especially when he had had a large dose of city life: "The country is a port from which one can look out upon all storms." [35] No one can stand upon the platform at Ferney and not feel that the man who picked that refuge for his old age had some appreciation of the larger aspects of natural beauty. And at moments this appreciation breaks out into a real, if brief, delight: "My dear friends, how lovely the country is: it gives a pleasure you know nothing about." [36] Or again he has a charming phrase like the following: "The streams, the flowers, and the woods console; too often men do not." [37] But in general he is too

44

busy to attend to such things, too full of plans and
jests, too much interested in men, whether consoling or amusing or exasperating, to bother with
streams and flowers. A page of Rousseau takes
you into a different world.

On the other hand, when it comes to books and
thinking, the eager mind is always alive, dips restlessly into everything, turns and twists ideas, mauls
them and plays with them and tears them with the
vivacity and velocity of a kitten or a young tiger.
Ignorant? Of course we are ignorant. It sometimes seems as if the more we read the more ignorant we are: "The world has become ignorant by
mere multiplicity of books." [38] Mistakes? Of
course we make mistakes. "If one is in error, why
not avow it?" [39] But it is all so vastly amusing, all,
all. Mathematics, indeed, are a little of a stumb-
ling-block. Madame du Châtelet likes them and
works hard over them, and therefore he works hard
over them. He begs a friend to send him something a little lighter, just to relieve these dismal
studies. Then he instantly retracts. Are there any
dismal studies? [40] To his quick, fertile, joyous
spirit indeed there were not. As for the natural
sciences, they were nothing but play. In his youth
he was infatuated with them, and he might have

45

been so all his life, if there had not been the Jesuits to deal with. "Now you might have a physical laboratory and get an expert to run it. It is one of the great amusements of life. We have a delightful one; but, alas, one has to leave such pleasant, quiet things as that." [41]

And literature proper was far more fascinating than even the physical sciences. Voltaire's delight in reading the great authors of many literatures, in commenting upon them and commending them, was inexhaustible. No doubt there was much about his judgment and taste that was narrow. Precisely because he was so intense and individual in his likings and dislikings he had often the appearance of prejudice and limitation. His pronouncement that Shakespeare was "a drunken savage" will always be quoted and considered as the extreme of Gallic incapacity for appreciating Anglo-Saxon idols. Yet in literature as in everything else, he had an extraordinary shrewdness and quickness of insight, and Sainte-Beuve remarks with perfect justice that when Voltaire is right he is right in an astonishing degree. Furthermore, in spite of his French limitations, he had a surprising breadth of judgment and sympathy in certain respects. How just is his comment on the defects of great writers:

46

"No man is without fault . . . It is not the great faults of petty people that we should emphasize, but the little faults of the great; for they are our models, and we are always in danger of imitating their weaker points." [42] Again, French as he was, no man was quicker to see the deficiencies of his countrymen, and much as he admired Corneille and Racine the artificial element of their work could not but impress him: "It is a strange prejudice with us Franks, that all the characters must have the same nobility of soul, that they must all be well bred, finely mannered, conventionally restrained: nature is not like that at all." [43] Even, in a passage which goes far to make up for the drunken savage, he points out that that strange Englishman had something which the genteel French dramatists never got: "This Gilles Shakespeare, with all his barbarity and absurdity, has, like Lope de Vega, touches so naïve and so true that all the reasonings of Pierre Corneille are frigid beside the tragedy of the said Gilles." [44] Finally, whether right or wrong, Voltaire had the gift of saying about authors, as about other things, the word that sticks; as in his remark on Ariosto, whom he adored, "people are always stealing volumes of my Ariosto; nobody ever stole my

47

Dante." [45]   Or about Petrarch, whom he calls "the most gifted genius of the world in the art of always saying the same thing." [46]

In abstract philosophy Voltaire's interest was somewhat less than in literature. His keen, direct spirit was impatient of mystery, of obscurity, and was perhaps too inclined to conclude that where he could not see there was nothing to be seen. He reiterates in different forms the celebrated bit in "Candide," "Of metaphysics he knew about what has been known in all ages, that is to say, very little." He wanted to be definite, to be positive, and in these elusive matters of thought there was little assurance of positiveness anywhere. "It is only charlatans who are certain." [47] He liked the name *philosophe,* liked to apply it to himself and his friends in the somewhat pedantic fashion of the eighteenth century, liked to write innumerable articles on so-called philosophical subjects for the Encyclopédie. But it was all rather practical in bent, and what was best in philosophy was hardly worthy of so high-sounding a term. "It is said that philosophy makes people happy; but my idea is that the people who said that had pretty good digestions." [48] At the same time it must not be assumed that because Voltaire was always clear, he

48

was always shallow. Clarity is an immense intellectual blessing, and may and most of all should be applied to those things that need it most; and clarity and profundity are not so incompatible as some persons not perfectly familiar with either are inclined to suppose. Above all, Voltaire at his better moments was quite capable of that large and dignified attitude toward life which perhaps has something more of philosophy in it than merely good digestion. How noble and just is his statement of this attitude: "Let us be philosophical at least in our latter days. Let us not employ them in sacrificing to the vanities of the world, in running after phantoms, in trying to escape from ourselves, in wasting our souls upon mere externals, in feeding upon wind." [49] Surely we have something besides the vain mocker here.

Yet in religion Voltaire was undeniably a good deal of a mocker. Superstition, empty fears, idols, mummeries, intolerance, cruelty irritated him, and in attacking them he was too apt to be regardless of the deeper and more important things that might be associated with them. His enormous power of raillery, his fierce, bitter, stinging tongue, ran riot with him and led him to excesses of indecent mocking, no doubt beyond his intentions and his better feeling. Then, when he felt that he had offended the temporal and spiritual powers past endurance, he professed to repent, professed conformity, built chapels, cajoled priests, made a half cynical ostentation of religion which was a worse mockery than the actual railing. And all the time he asserted, and perhaps believed, that he was quarreling only with the artificial, the conventional, and the false. The *Infâme,* which he and his friends attacked so furiously, was certainly not understood by them to be the personality of Jesus, or even any element of good and godlike in what he represented; it was simply the corruptions and distortions, doctrinal and moral, which had grown up under cover of that vast earthly organism, the Catholic Church. Voltaire affirmed and reaffirmed his belief in God, not only formally, but in casual phrases, which meant far more, "For me, who believe in God as much and more than any one." [50] Nevertheless, it is manifestly impossible to represent him or think of him as a devout believer. But it would be far from just to look upon him as an incarnate Mephistopheles, a spirit who denies, and nothing else. He was too busy with actual living, too intensely, vividly dynamic in the present to bother with affairs of merely ultimate concern. Let them wait: you have got to live now.

There was one thing, at any rate, in which he was not negative, and which expressed and fulfilled his vitality most of all: that was writing and the pen. From his youth to his age he was a writer, and to pour out literature was as instinctive with him as breathing. It made little difference what the circumstances were, he wrote just the same. Whether he was ill or well, glad or sorry, at home and abroad, alone and with men and women crowding about him, still the pen moved, still the words came, without cessation, almost without repose: it was his life. Nor did it make much difference what he wrote. Few authors have been so universal. Epic poetry, pompously solemn or gaily indecent; quick, light society verses, tragedy, comedy, history, biography, fiction, grave essays and blighting satire, it was all one to him. He could do all of them, and all of them well, and the product fills fifty solid volumes. His pen would have danced on and on to the end of the world, and he would have gaily recorded even that final disaster for the benefit of cosmic posterity, or just for pure fun.

It is evident that to achieve such an immense total a man must work quickly and easily. Prob-

ably no man ever threw off words and thoughts
with more fire and petulance than Voltaire. His
pen flew, or, when age and infirmity obliged him to
dictate, his tongue flew, and always with the same
unfailing facility. His theme descended upon him
and possessed him, and for the time he was lost in
it. Take his tragedies. They seem to us today
somewhat artificial and decidedly melodramatic.
Yet even today they retain a touch of the immense
vitality that he poured into them. And he did pour
it in. Listen to his whirlwind account of the composition of one of them: "I hunted up all that great
names have that is most imposing, all that the secret
religion of the ancients . . . had in it that was
terrible or consoling, all that torments us in the
passions, all the vanity and the wretchedness of
human grandeur, and all the ruinous disaster of
human misfortune. The subject seized upon me
with such violence that I wrote the whole play in
six days, counting a little of the nights." [51]

It would naturally be supposed that a speed of
production like this would involve defects of haste
and carelessness. Nothing can be further from the
truth. It was rare indeed that an imperfect sentence left Voltaire's pen. And this came first from
the long habit and instinct of the natural writer.

52

His language was clear, direct, vivid, and forcible because his thoughts were. At the same time he was not only a rapid but a most conscientious worker. He poured out his first draughts with speed and facility, but he corrected them with minute patience and care. Verses must be without flaw: "If there is the least fault in construction, if a conjunction is forgotten, if the exactly right word is not used, or not used in its proper place, you may conclude that the jewel of your thought is not well set. And be sure that verses which have one of these faults will never linger in men's hearts, will not be re-read and remembered: it is only the perfect verses that are retained and loved." [52] With prose he was almost equally punctilious. He revised and worked over and polished till all possible suggestion of slovenliness was disposed of forever.

Even, he endured the last test of a writer's patience: he not only corrected himself but listened with humility to the corrections of others. He submits his work to his friends, asks for suggestions, asks with a singular self-effacement: "Encourage me all you can, for I am docile as a child." [53] And if he was at times a petulant and wayward child, in this point he seems earnest and sincere.

He debates the suggestions that are made to him, considers them, and occasionally adopts them—which is a good deal when you know the nature of the writing tribe.

The truth is that he deferred to the opinion of others because he passionately desired their praise and to do things that they would praise. It is true that, like other authors and artists, he at times disclaims all regard for popular applause. He is working for higher things. But the applause delighted him; all the same, was necessary to him; he fed upon it, lived upon it and, when it failed or was in any way flawed, he was restless, uneasy, and discontent. "What endless pains and toil for the vain breath of glory! Yet without this chimæra what should we do? It is as necessary to the soul as food is to the body." [54] And glory came upon him immensely, involved him, transfigured him—glory direct, and the envy and abuse which are an almost equally delightful inverted form of glory. Few writers, except perhaps Goethe, have been more adored and especially talked about in their ripe old age.

But great as the glory naturally was, it was never enough, and Voltaire himself used all sorts of means to broaden and intensify it. He was always writing anonymous squibs and satires to startle and stimulate and shock. Consequently, innumerable disreputable things of a similar nature were fastened upon him, and he was always disclaiming them, quarreling with the editors who printed them, and generally keeping up an atmosphere of magnificent turbulence which fostered the glory, or at any rate the publicity, and made life full of excitement and, for a temper like his, of variegated charm.

Through it all it must be admitted that he shows an extraordinary susceptibility and vanity, which are often contemptible. Yet it is hard to condemn them altogether, or at any rate him. He dodged and cheated and lied and stole. Oh, yes, very likely. But he did it all in the most winning simplicity of spirit. Here again one notes something peculiarly childlike about him, as there was about the vanity of Cicero, though they were both rather sophisticated children. And nobody knew better than Voltaire the emptiness of literary triumph, or any other triumph: "Sometimes I think of all I have gone through, and I conclude that, if I had a son who was to go through the same, I would wring his neck out of sheer paternal tenderness." [55] Yet in reality he would not have missed a single torment of it all; or, as Viola puts it in "The Coxcomb," with more discernment and more charm:

"I'll tell my daughters then
The miseries their mother had in love,
And say, "My girls, be wiser!" yet I would not
Have had more wit myself." [56]

IV

If Voltaire's vitality pours itself out in his writings generally, it is perhaps most of all manifest in his correspondence. The bulk of the letters we have were written in age; yet the fire and fury inspire and animate every line of them. "I have never been able to understand how anybody could be cold: that is too much for me." [57] Could a man paint himself better in a brief sentence? The vitality sparkles and glitters in the unceasing, unfailing wit; not humor, the vitality did not permit that, it was incompatible with the remoteness and detachment of the humorous attitude; but the wit makes the pages glow and crackle like a great Aurora. To be sure, Voltaire said of himself, "as for comedies, I won't meddle with them: I am a tragic animal"; [58] and this time one feels that he has not hit it so well as usual, though one understands what he meant. To live is perhaps tragedy, and he lived, if ever man did. But what counts most of all in the letters is that he said what he thought, threw off shackles, broke restraints, let his spirit and his life flow out to whoever would listen to him. The results may be sometimes dangerous, not to say indecent, but they are always revealing, always human, and, why not admit, fascinating also. "My vocation is to say what I think, *fari quae sentiam.*" [59]

Taken altogether, the correspondence of Voltaire is perhaps the most wonderful, and certainly one of the most extensive in the world. It has not the imagination of Flaubert or the unearthly grace of Lamb, but for vigor and variety it is unequaled. He often speaks of writing ten or twelve letters a day, and though many of them were dictated, this does not seem to make any difference in their power or their charm. It was the brain that did it, not the fingers. His correspondents included people of the greatest note and importance of any in his time; not only kings and queens but great poets, great artists, great scholars, and great actors. Though he writes differently to different ones, and perhaps with more intimate and stimulated freedom to those whom he likes best, as D'Argental or Madame du Deffand, he writes to all with equal energy and equal surprising diversity and originality of thought and phrase. As the later and better editions include the letters of his correspondents as well as his own, of Frederick and Catherine, of Diderot and D'Alembert, the whole forms one of the most remarkable epitomes of a historical period that can well be imagined.

Yet the external matters, vividly and brilliantly treated as they are, are less interesting than the revelation of the man himself; and few human beings, hardly even Pepys, have laid themselves more largely and completely bare to the curious gaze of posterity. The chief, magnificent agent in accomplishing this is, no doubt, style, and it is difficult to exaggerate the great qualities of Voltaire as a stylist, even if imaginative richness is not among them. Unfailing clarity, absolute precision and exactitude, are a small part of it. Beyond these there is a subtle secret of rhythm especially, such as Swift had, a power of adapting all the cunning possibilities of utterance to the thing to be uttered, of bringing out the infinite resources of words in color and accent in such a way as to drive the thought home and make it stick, that has been possessed by few other writers in any language.

And note that Voltaire is never a rhetorician, never preoccupied, as is Macaulay, with the effect or the making of his own phrases. It is all a matter of thought and feeling; only, by some wonderful instinctive gift the thought and feeling pour themselves out in a form which is masterfully and imperishably the best.

Still, Voltaire's revelation of himself is not merely an affair of utterance. It is far more a question and a manifestation of that superb vitality on which we have all along insisted. There is no other correspondence in the world in which the writer so constantly, so incessantly keeps himself before us. The odd thing is that, with this there is so little impression of egotism, at any rate far less than with Cicero or Swift. There is none of the monotony that results from Madame de Sévigné's tedious iteration of her daughter. Voltaire's letters turn perpetually from one thing to another and touch with the largest variety on all subjects in the universe. But these subjects are somehow intimately related to the writer, seen through the medium of that vivid, glowing, sparkling spirit of Voltaire. He draws all things to himself, and again he diffuses himself with the most vital eagerness into the essential movement of all things. So intense is the impression of this that you grow to feel yourself nearer to him than to any personal friend and, while you often smile at him and sometimes sigh over him, as for that matter you do over your friends, you constantly wonder, and in the end you feel something distinctly approaching affection.

III
THOMAS GRAY

CHRONOLOGY

Thomas Gray

Born, London, December 26, 1716.

Went to Cambridge, 1734

Traveled abroad, 1739-1741

Elegy published, 1751

Appointed professor of modern history and modern languages
at Cambridge, 1768

Died, Cambridge, July 30, 1771

THOMAS GRAY

I

SECLUSION and solitude, thought and thought, and a little or a great deal of reading, and more thought; quiet days and quiet nights steeped in tranquillity, saturated with reflection, and not unduly bereft of peaceful slumber—such, in the crowded middle years of the eighteenth century was the life of Thomas Gray. He was born in 1716, of a good family, with moderate means, went through the usual routine of English education at Eton and Cambridge, made a few close friends and a certain number of Latin verses, frolicked a little, with more or less distaste, toiled for some time at law with a distaste that was even greater. Then he abandoned worldly usefulness, unless a professor's appointment during his last years can be called such, and shut himself up in dim Cambridge chambers with dim, piled books and dim, piled thoughts; hoped a little, regretted a little, dreamed vastly, wrote a little great poetry, and slipped away into the dimmer, larger silence in 1771.

Naturally Gray's life was not quite all solitude and introspection. What life could be? There were gleams of external movement and diversity when he roved shyly through the great world, astonished at its senseless clatter. After his university education was finished he went abroad with his schoolfellow, Horace Walpole, and spent some months in France and Italy. Walpole's curiosity was inexhaustible. He wanted to see everybody and do everything, and Gray trailed his weary indolence after his friend's eager vivacity. In letters to those at home the lonely scholar described their parti-colored doings, sometimes with moderate zest, sometimes with evident fretfulness. He writes a jocose itinerary to Wharton,[1] with a vivid enumeration of great sights and little annoyances. There are people, endless people, some amusing, more tedious. There are wolves on the slopes of the mountains and bores in the cities. There is trifling and dancing and laughing. There are cathedrals and pictures and bad inns and worse roads and hurly-burly remote enough from the academic peace of Cambridge. Then the two friends chafed each other and parted. It is easy to see why without going into special reasons. The close intimacy of travel is always too apt to breed friction. Walpole was rich, spoiled, the son of a prime minister. Gray was nobody, and proud as the devil. What happened was bound to happen. In later days the quarrel was patched up; but for the time they separated and Gray was probably well pleased to return to solitude and silence.

In the thirty years after this of course there were many breaks, longer or shorter. Like every Englishman, Gray was often in London, not often enough to love it or to feel at home in it, but with occasional visits which made him sufficiently familiar with its sights and its throngs and its noise and bustle and hurry. If there was a striking event, like a coronation, he was curious enough to record the press of great people, with their blaze of show and splendor and their unfailing petty humanity through it all. He was too indolent or too indifferent to go himself to the places of diversion, Ranelagh or Vauxhall, but he commented with sarcastic interest on the manners and motives of those who did go: "So they go to Vauxhall; well, but is not it a very great design, very new, finely lighted, well, yes, ay, very fine truly, so they yawn and go to Vauxhall, and then it's too hot, and then it's too

cold, and here's a wind, and there's a damp, and
so the women go to bed, and the men to a ——
house. . . . However, to do us justice, I think we
are a reasonable, but by no means a pleasurable
people; and to mend us we must have a dash of the
French and Italian; yet I don't know how." [2]

Then there is the opera, and this is more worth
while, yes, even takes him out of himself, in spite of
the crowds and the dirt and the fatigue. "But
then the Burlettas and the Paganina. I have not
been so pleased with anything these many years.
. . . She has not the invention, the fire, and the
variety of action, that the Spiletta had; yet she is
light, agile, ever in motion, and above all graceful;
but then her voice, her ear, her taste in singing: Good God!—as Mr. Richardson the painter
says." [3] So London yielded something to take
back into the Cambridge quiet.

Or there were leisurely trips through the lovely
English country. It was hard to pack and get
started, harder and harder as the years went on;
but it paid, after a fashion, with what it left in
memory at any rate. You chose the long summer
days, visited friends in the north, south, east, or
west, even stretched your touring fancy as far as
the wilder districts of Scotland. Walpole was

THOMAS GRAY

always busy with the toy magnificence of Strawberry Hill, and after their trouble was adjusted and Gray had become a person of some distinction, his old friend was glad to see him and to get the benefit of his sure and delicate taste about some bit of quaint ornamentation or curious furnishing. Walpole's press also issued some of Gray's poems, and there had to be consultations about details here.

Moreover, Gray was a thorough archæologist and antiquarian, and in his journeys he was always eager to inspect old castles and churches, to examine monuments and decipher inscriptions, to classify and enjoy rare specimens of Gothic architecture and Renaissance painting. In all these investigations one is struck with the minute, exact conscientiousness of the man's spirit. To be sure, the studies may not be worth while. What studies really are worth while? But, out of respect to oneself, if one is going into them at all, let us be careful and complete. "The drift of my present studies, is to know, wherever I am, what lies within reach, that may be worth seeing, whether it be building, ruin, park, garden, prospect, picture, or monument; to whom it does, or has belonged, and what has been the characteristic and taste of different ages. You will say, this is the object of all antiquaries, but pray, what antiquary ever saw these objects in the same light, or desired to know them for a like reason?" [4] So he notes and marks and lists and distinguishes, and is occupied if not happy.

Also, there is the element of nature in these rambling excursions, as well as the element of human production and association, and Gray is perhaps even more at home in the former. When he was fairly started on a pilgrimage he displayed an amount of energy one would have hardly looked for in a person of such sedentary habits. He drives for long hours over rough roads, climbs steep and difficult slopes, puts up with petty inconveniences, all for the sake of seeing some picturesque site or unfrequented stream or summit. He even approves of movement for itself: "Do not you think a man may be the wiser (I had almost said the better) for going a hundred or two of miles; and that the mind has more room in it than most people seem to think, if you will but furnish the apartments?" [5] He enjoys the ocean, "where the sea appears glittering through the shade, and vessels, with their white sails, that glide across and are lost again." [6] He enjoys an exquisite boating-trip on the River Wye.[7] He enjoys an autumn in Scotland, in spite of the draw-backs, which he sets forth with humorous vividness: "Then I had so beautiful an autumn, Italy could hardly produce a nobler scene, and this so sweetly contrasted with that perfection of nastiness, and total want of accommodation that Scotland only can supply. Oh, you would have blessed yourself. I shall certainly go again; what a pity it is I cannot draw, nor describe, nor ride on horseback." [8]

But from such little, brief wanderings in the wide, untraveled world there is always a quick return, a return no doubt laden with richly garnered food for the inward eye, but still the same re-entrance into cloistered solitude. Sometimes the return comes with regret, regret even of the little inconveniences that for the moment perturb the tranquil surface of life: "In Cambridge there is nothing so troublesome as that one has nothing to trouble one." [9] Sometimes the renewal of peace and privacy brings just a large sense of relief for, after all, one is a creature of habit and gets so easily rooted and, oh, so permanently: " 'Tis true Cambridge is very ugly, she is very dirty, and very dull; but I'm like a cabbage, where I'm stuck, I love to grow; you should pull me up sooner than any one, but I shall be ne'er the

better for transplanting." [10]   And so the seclusion and remoteness increase with the increasing
years.

II

Yet seclusion does not necessarily mean self-
absorption. The most extreme eremite, if he is to
keep his sanity, must get away from his surroundings, spiritually if not physically. And sometimes
when the feet never move the spirit maintains the
widest and most restless outlook. After all, one
is human and there is a great, tempting, puzzling
human world about one. One must touch it occasionally, one must look at it and listen to it. Even
it may be that the vision and the sensibility are
made more keen by remoteness, dreamy and in a
certain sense abstract, but wider, more equable, and
more penetrating.

And so Gray looked around him constantly, sent
his gaze far abroad from that quiet, dull Cambridge atmosphere and surveyed the strange doings
of men, rather dreamily, as if it were all no concern
of his, but with a searching curiosity and sometimes
with amusement, sometimes with dread. Events of
history or politics? In the past you could probe
them with an antiquarian's zeal and, if they would

70

feed nothing else they would feed the restless activity of an unoccupied mind. As to any comfort to be derived from the contemplation of them, well, there might be two views: "I am not altogether of your opinion as to your historical consolation in time of trouble. A calm melancholy it may produce, a stiller sort of despair . . . but I doubt no real content or comfort can ever arise in the human mind but from hope." [11] But what most impressed you when you saw the past in its proper perspective was the terrible insignificance of great people and great doings. There was such a huge bustle, such a tempestuous stir for a few short years. Then it was forgotten, and the kings and queens slept in the dust beside the peasants. Would it not be exactly so with the noisy tumult that went on immediately about one? Frederick was a great king. Wolfe was a brave soldier. They both must die, like you and me, and there was an end of it. King George was crowned, and jeweled throngs swept and glittered through the tedious ceremonies. The earth opened at Lisbon, and shrieking throngs were engulfed in it. But oblivion would engulf them all at last. You wondered a little, you pitied a little, you smiled a little. Then you turned back to your books.

71

In the obscure, profound humanitarian movement which was just beginning to stir the conventional eighteenth century, Gray seems to have
taken little interest.   He disliked the French
philosophers and all their doings.   Social and
economic questions did not appeal to him.   He had
all the traditional English gentleman's aversion to
commerce and commercial affairs.   He reads a
book on "The Manners of the Times" and remarks,
"There is one thing in it I applaud, which is the
dissertation against trade, for I have always said
it was the ruin of the nation." [12]   If he had lived
to see the great upheaval in France, it is easy to
imagine what he would have thought of it.

On the other hand, the little daily doings of men
and women, the quick play and interchange of their
passions and hopes and fears, interested and amused
him inexhaustibly. As so often happens with such
solitary figures who have little active life of their
own, he liked to supply the lack with the experiences of others.   When he was young he wrote,
"For my part, I could entertain myself this month
merely with the common streets and the people in
them." [13]   The power of extracting such entertainment did not decrease with age.

He liked a bit of gossip or scandal.   Though he

lived so much by himself, he knew the world of society and its doings, or knew of them, and such anecdotes as Walpole was always collecting diverted him immensely. He had his own comments on them; shrewd, quick, and vivid; sometimes cutting and bitter. Not that he was really ill-natured; he was not, was capable of much kindly, active sympathy. But the pretence of the world annoyed him, and the shallowness of the world disgusted him. When a scene or conjuncture of circumstances excites his wrath, his sarcastic account of it is not to be forgotten: "We were—a man that writes for Lord Royston; a man that writes for Dr. Burton of York; a third that writes for the Emperor of Germany, or Dr. Pocock, for he speaks the worst English I ever heard; Dr. Stukely, who writes for himself, the very worst person he could write for; and I, who only read to know if there were anything worth writing, and that not without some difficulty." [14]

When he comes to deal with the men and things immediately about him in academic Cambridge, his words do take on a flavor of bitterness which seems at times a little unnecessary. One is reminded of Heine's cruel branding of the university life of Göttingen. "Cambridge is a delight of a place now there is nobody in it. I do believe you would like it, if you knew what it was without inhabitants." [15] As to said inhabitants, his comment is too often such as he makes on Dr. Chapman: "Our friend Dr. Chapman (one of its nuisances) is not expected here again in a hurry. He is gone to his grave with five fine mackerel in his belly. He ate them all at one dinner; but his fate was a turbot on Trinity Sunday, of which he left little for the company besides bones. . . . They say he made a very good end." [16]

Yet in Cambridge, as everywhere else in the world, it was necessary not only to observe men but to come into direct contact with them, and this was less suited to Gray's taste. There was daily practical contact, business contact. No matter how much you may hate trade, you have to live, have to live under cover and dress and eat. To do these things you have to have money and spend it. Gray's income was unearned and small and sure; but he had to draw it and handle it and mix with those who furnished the things he needed. His general remarks on money matters are touched with the humor approaching cynicism which colored so much of his comment on life: "It is a foolish thing that one can't only not live as one pleases, but

where and with whom one pleases, without money.
Swift somewhere says that money is liberty; and I
fear money is friendship too and society, and almost
every external blessing. It is a great though ill-
natured comfort to see most of those who have it in
plenty without pleasure, without liberty, and without friends." [17] No one can question, however,
that Gray understood the two great essentials so
far as money is concerned: order and thoughtfulness. It is clear that he was careful in his expendi-
ture and strictly honorable in all his dealings.
That he was charitable, for his means, is also to be
taken for granted, though he was the last man to
boast of it. His touching phrase as to poverty
sounds absolutely sincere: "There is but one real
evil in it . . . and that is that you have less the
power of assisting others who have not the same
resources to support them." [18]

And contact with humanity could not be quite
confined to matters of business. Purely social relations were desirable, as even Gray would have
admitted, and, whether desirable or not, they were
often unavoidable. But he did not take to them.
In appearance he was a little, trim, tidy person,
very dignified, rather conventional, rather unap-
proachable, and few indeed were those who suc-

ceeded in approaching him. Walpole said of him:
"He is the worst company in the world,—from a
melancholy turn, from living reclusely, and from
a little too much dignity, he never converses easily
. . . his writings are admirable; he himself is not
agreeable." [19] That there were times when he
could be gay and unbend, even in early days enter
into a frolic, is evident from his letters; for example from his description of the wild doings at
Rheims in 1739.[20] No doubt at all times he could
chat with a friend over a late fire, delightfully.
As with most proud, self-conscious people, his own
monstrous, intrusive, inexplicable self was always
getting between him and those to whom he wished
to come nearest. "People in high spirits and
gayety overpower me and entirely take away mine.
I can yet be diverted with their sallies, but if they
appear to take notice of my dullness, it sinks me
to nothing." [21] And the conclusion of it all is,
"As to humanity, you know my aversion to it;
which is barbarous and inhuman, but I cannot help
it. God forgive me!" [22]

In a life so organized and so guided one would
not expect to find the influence of women very conspicuous. To Gray they were remote, puzzling,
most embarrassing creatures, evidently useful,

probably estimable, but not to be sought for daily comfort or converse. "For me, I am come to my resting-place, and find it very necessary, after living for a month in a house with three women that laughed from morning to night, and would allow nothing to the sulkiness of my disposition. Company and cards at home, parties by land and water abroad, and (what they call) *doing something,* that is, racketing about from morning to night, are occupations, I find, that wear out my spirits." [23] The ideal of those quiet chambers in Pembroke Hall, Cambridge, was certainly not to do nothing, but at any rate not to "racket about." As domestic appurtenances, especially in childhood, women of course had their advantage, and one carried forever a certain tender association with them. "Poor Mrs. Bonfoy (who taught me to pray) is dead." [24] For a touch it goes deep, does it not? And there is the exquisite word to Nicholls, written in age, about the loss of a mother: "I had discovered a thing very little known, which is, that in one's whole life one never can have any more than a single mother. . . . I never discovered this . . . till it was too late. It is 13 years ago, and seems but yesterday, and every day I live, it sinks deeper into my heart." [25]

As for love in the more ordinary sense, there
may have been unrecorded passions in youth, but
there is no hint of them in Gray's letters. Gray
speaks of the marriage of his friends with respect,
with curiosity, with his usual gracious playfulness:
"I rejoice; but has she common-sense? Is she a
gentlewoman? Has she money? Has she a nose?
I know she sings a little and twiddles on the harpsi-
chord. . . . Adieu, I am truly yours. I hope her
hair is not red though." [26] For himself, he refers
to the conjugal state with neither congratulation
nor regret.

All the affection that should have gone to wife
and children was poured out on friends. Even
here perhaps it was difficult to do the pouring by
word of mouth. But from the quiet chambers you
could send warm, delightful, humorous letters
which in a shy way might suggest something of
what you felt. To be sure, the reserve haunted
the letters also, that confounded, strange restraint
which made it impossible to give entirely what one
would most have liked to bestow. It is a remote,
secluded world; and perhaps a quaint dim Cambridge corner, after all, shuts you off no more than
the repellent, conventional friendliness of the noisy
crowd. But you can love your friends and cherish

them and, in vague, uncertain, ineffective written words you can strive to tell them so. There is West, there is Wharton, there is Mason; one's love for them is at least something real in a motley medley of delusive, evasive shadows. Oh, one sees their faults well enough when one has those keen eyes that see the faults of everything. There is the dilatory Mason, whose "greatest wants do not make him move a foot the faster, nor has he properly speaking anything one can call a passion about him, except a little malice and revenge." [27] But what are faults to love? And in one's old age one inclines with singular craving to the caressing tenderness of youth, one yearns for the honest flattery of a Nicholls or a Bonstetten, and one even at last likes to cherish the delusion that those fretting barriers may be overcome and one can reveal bare soul when one wishes it, as well as when one does not: "It is impossible for me to dissemble with you; such as I am I expose my heart to your view, nor wish to conceal a single thought rom your penetrating eyes." [28] For love, after all, is but the straining for the unattainable.

III

And as humanity offered its mighty, though forever tantalizing refuge and solace from the overpowering absorption in one's own soul, so there were other forms of refuge in the abstract, detached resources of thought and contemplation. There was art. Gray delighted in Italian and other painting, studied it in such opportunities as he had and made fruitful and suggestive comments upon it. Architecture charmed him. Old Gothic ruins had a peculiar fascination for his melancholy and slightly ruinous temperament. He liked the more decorative forms of art also, advised Walpole and others about the purchase of stained glass and tapestries, and spent long, unprofitable hours in the investigation of such things. Especially he enjoyed music, and played the piano of his day sufficiently to get the richest artistic inspiration that the solitary dreamer can create for himself. He writes to Mason of some lessons for the pianoforte by Carlo Bach: "Mr. Neville and the old musicians here do not like them, but to me they speak not only music, but passion. I cannot play them, though they are not hard; yet I make a smattering that serves 'to deceive my solitary days.'" [29]

Gray's relation to external nature is especially interesting because of the reflection of it in his poetry. He was always keenly alive to the changes and the manifestations of the natural world, kept careful notes of temperature and weather, made elaborate lists of the arrival of birds and the leafing and budding of flowers. He delighted in gardens and his friends thought he understood the planting of them.[30] Probably he did, though he was not a man to overrate his own powers in any line: "Reasonable people know themselves better than is commonly imagined."[31] He sighs with real pathos for horticultural delights which he cannot share: "And so you have a garden of your own, and you plant and transplant, and are dirty and amused. Are not you ashamed of yourself? Why, I have no such thing, you monster: nor ever shall be either dirty or amused as long as I live. My gardens are in the window, like those of a lodger up three pair of stairs in Petticoat-Lane or Camomile-Street, and they go to bed regularly under the same roof that I do."[32]

As to the wild outdoors, it must be admitted that Gray never quite got the touch, because he never quite had the feeling, of the romantic writers of fifty years later. At his best he hardly reaches

81

even the depth of Collins's "simple bell" or the tenderness of Cowper's primroses. Yet the direct sincerity and power of the lines in the Vicissitude Ode give something nowhere to be found in the wide desert of Pope's cleverness:

> "The meanest floweret of the vale,
>   The simplest note that swells the gale,
>   The common sun, the air, the skies,
>   To him are opening Paradise."

In the enjoyment of mountain scenery Gray curiously represents the transition between the old Latin dislike of the rugged, the dangerous, the terrible, and the more subtle passion of the nineteenth century poets. To the shy recluse of level Cambridge the Alps, and in a less degree the Scottish Highlands, represented a delicious shudder; they were strange, they were picturesque, above all they were full of literature: "In our little journey up to the Grande Chartreuse, I do not remember to have gone ten paces without an exclamation that there was no restraining. Not a precipice, not a torrent, not a cliff, but is pregnant with religion and poetry." [33] We have still some way to go to the dreaming of Obermann in the high and lonely valleys or to Byron's outcry,

"And to me
High mountains are a feeling." [34]

Besides the æsthetic distractions the recluse had always the diversion of speculative thought, if he cared to make use of it. When he was in the first mild sparkle of youth such things seemed rather dull to him. "Must I plunge into metaphysics? Alas, I cannot see in the dark: nature has not furnished me with the optics of a cat. Must I pore upon mathematics? Alas, I cannot see in too much light: I am no eagle. It is very possible that two and two make four, but I would not give four farthings to demonstrate this ever so clearly; and if these be the profits of life, give me the amusements of it." [35] Later perhaps, when the amusements palled, the wide paths of reflection may have taken on something more of charm. Yet it is evident that Gray was never a passionate or a tormented abstract thinker. His own statement of the matter is, no doubt, much too modest: "a reasonable quantity of dulness, a great deal of silence, and something that rather resembles than is, thinking." [36] Still, the sleepy air of the east of England probably increased a natural disposition to indolence, and it seemed easier to turn aside from great problems than to wrestle with them, to ac-

cept and cherish traditional belief and worship
rather than to dispute. Moreover, Gray by nature
was conservative. Radicalism in politics he ab-
horred, and radicalism in philosophy was, to say
the least, very distasteful. Voltaire he detested,
and French speculative ventures in general seemed
to him mainly dangerous and always unprofitable:
"Their atheism is a little too much, too shocking
to rejoice at. I have long been sick at it in their
authors, and hated them for it; but I pity their
poor innocent people of fashion. They were bad
enough when they believed everything." [37]

Minute and technical scholarship was far better
than theoretical divagations. You could lose yourself in old authors, you could discuss and debate
texts and readings, you could compare the opinion
of one dusty pedant with that of another dusty
pedant, and though you knew that the pedants were
dead and their opinions of no value whatever, even
to the moths and spiders, it all sufficed to make the
heavy-footed hours tread a little more lightly. In
the thickening twilight of a dull November after-
noon it might seem a little dull. There were people out in the world who were loving and hating
and laughing. Sometimes one's heart quivered at
the thought of joining them. But no doubt their

love and their laughter were dull also, for November afternoons are dull everywhere. So one returns to the dusty pedants, and does what one can to satisfy an unappeasable habit of accuracy and minute detail, and forgets, or falls asleep.

To be sure, there were forms of literature less soporific than dusty pedantry and Gray touched and tried them all; for if a somewhat desultory reader, he was a vast one. When Nicholls expressed surprise at the extent of his reading, the modest answer was: "Why should you be surprised, for I do nothing else?" [38] He enjoyed the imaginative writers of the past. Racine was a delight to him and he was unwilling to hear him criticized: "I don't know what to say to you with regard to Racine: it sounds to me as if anybody should fall upon Shakespeare, who indeed lies infinitely more open to criticism of all kinds, but I should not care to be the person that undertook it." [39]

Also, he read everything notable that came from his contemporaries, and commented on it with frankness and shrewdness and sometimes with enthusiasm. He did not, indeed, care much for the verdict of the great multitude of readers and the selling of a best-seller struck him as not very substantial: "I wonder to hear you ask the opinion of a nation, where those who pretend to judge don't judge at all; and the rest (the wiser part) wait to catch the judgment of the world immediately above them, that is, Dick's Coffee-House, and the Rainbow: so that the readier way would be to ask Mrs. This and Mrs. T'other, that keeps the bar there." [40] But he admired and enjoyed as well as criticized much that was admired by others. He found Rousseau's "Nouvelle Héloise" a bore,[41] as did Voltaire; but the "Emile" interested and impressed him greatly.[42] Montesquieu he praised with real enthusiasm.[43]

To one remark of Montesquieu at least he would probably have been as willing to subscribe as any one can be. Can it have been quite true of Montesquieu himself? "I never had a sorrow which a half-hour's reading could not dissipate." And if there was any kind of literature which could produce such a delightful effect, Gray would certainly have said it was fiction. He loved to read novels. Those of us who today find the mystery-story one of the greatest blessings of the world could not perhaps read the novels that Gray read; but we can understand fully the general significance of his remark: "Now as the paradisiacal pleasures of the

Mahometans consist in playing upon the flute and lying with houris, be mine to read eternal new romances of Marivaux and Crébillon." [44]

Where one reads so much there must be sometimes the temptation to write. Where one has such days and years of idleness, one must sometimes get to regard work as a pleasure, and the only kind of work that attracted Gray was writing. As to the importance of work, the value of it, the satisfaction of it, his opinion was very decided, whatever may have been his practice. He bewailed his own indolence: "You need not fear unraveling my web. I am a sort of spider; and have little else to do but spin it over again, or creep to some other place and spin there. Alas! For one who has nothing to do but amuse himself, I believe my amusements are as little amusing as most folks'. But no matter: it makes the hours pass." [45] He envied and admired industry: "To be employed is to be happy." [46] He would have liked to write great works and to give his time and his life to it. But it was not a matter of wishing. He simply sat unproductive the larger part of his days and the great work refused to come: "It is the result (I suppose) of a certain disposition of mind, which does not depend on oneself, and which I have not felt this long time." [47]

To be sure, what he did produce was labored over with huge effort and pains. He could at times toss off a trifle, like the "Cat" and "The Long Story"; but the few great Odes and the "Elegy" received the utmost labor of revision and polishing. The extreme subtlety and delicacy of his extensive comments on the writing which his friends submitted to him prove sufficiently the days and nights of anxious thought which he must have devoted to his own. And the excision of the delicious omitted stanza of the "Elegy" shows what sacrifices a conscientious artist is ready to make to produce a masterpiece. Gray unquestionably belongs, with Leopardi and Flaubert, to the group of writers who are unwilling to let anything leave their hands till it is absolutely perfect. Even, perfection seems so shadowy and unachievable that they are often reluctant to part with their work at all.

One asks oneself naturally how much interest had Gray, who had so little interest in anything, in the future of these masterpieces to which he gave so many hours of thought and toil. Did he care for glory or seek for it? His obvious anxiety as to a possible professorship shows that he was not

wholly without the little human ambitions.[48]   The
indifference of the public annoyed him, as it does
the rest of us: "As your acquaintance in the
University (you say) do me the honor to admire,
it would be ungenerous in me not to give them
notice that they are doing a very unfashionable
thing, for all people of condition are agreed not
to admire, nor even to understand." [49]   Or again,
"Mr. Fox, supposing the Bard sung his song but
once over, does not wonder if Edward the First
did not understand him.   This last criticism is
rather unhappy, for though it had been sung a
hundred times under his window, it was absolutely
impossible King Edward should understand him;
but that is no reason for Mr. Fox, who lives almost
500 years after him.   It is very well; the next thing
I print shall be in Welsh—that's all." [50]   These
quaint little susceptibilities are to be expected
among the charms and graces of authorship.

Yet in the main Gray, like some others, pro-
claimed his disregard for success, at least for popularity.   He refused the laureateship, which many
satirize but few decline.   And he declared that he
had "no relish for any other fame than what is
conferred by the few real judges that are so thinly
scattered over the face of the earth." [51]

IV

At any rate, the echo of praise came but dimly into those secluded halls and quiet streets, where the living flitted about so casually among the mighty relics of the dead that no one could take their flattery or their blame or any of their pursuits with enduring seriousness. Somehow Gray's solitude takes one back to old Burton, who did but typify the life of so many English scholars, if it could be called life—the immense, remote detachment from all those great and petty things that tease and tempt and occupy the common herd of men. And as Burton distilled from his solitude a vast folio volume of melancholy, so Gray extracted from his a quaint melancholy of his own, compounded of many simples like that of Jaques in "As You Like It," broken and variegated with exquisite trifles and playfulness; dainty, shifting, vanishing, elusive, but still haunting and absorbing, with the suggestion of life flitting away, of slow days and swift years passing and nothing done with them, of the deceitfulness of hope, the emptiness of thought, the terrible imminence of the grave and something beyond it—all common topics enough but intensified by the drag of gray days and gray reflections.

The melancholy made sheer nonsense relishable and of delicate savor: "You forget Mr. Senhouse's acoustic warming-pan: we are in a hurry, for I cannot speak to him till it comes. God bless you, come and bring it with you, for we are as merry as the day is short. The squire is gone; he gave us a goose and a turkey, and two puddings of a moderate size." [52] You laughed at others and you laughed at yourself: "I keep an owl in the garden as like me as it can stare; only I do not eat raw meat, nor bite people by the fingers." [53] But still, still, as with Burton, that black-robed goddess Melancholy is waiting round the corner, spreads her quiet smothering pall over the gayest hopes and the wittiest associates. She comes in youth: "Low spirits are my true and faithful companions; they get up with me, go to bed with me, make journeys and returns as I do; nay, and pay visits, and will even affect to be jocose, and force a feeble laugh with me; but most commonly we sit alone together, and are the prettiest insipid company in the world." [54] She does not fail in age: "Your letter has made me happy, as happy as so gloomy, so solitary a being as I am is capable of being made." [55]

There has been some dispute over the quality of

Gray's melancholy. Matthew Arnold held that it was a blight brought upon him by the discord between the richness of his natural genius and the conventional habit of the eighteenth century. Tovey, who adored the eighteenth century, denied this and maintained that Gray's natural disposition would have been the same at any time. Lowell suggested that "Gray's melancholy was in part remorse at (if I may not say the waste) the abeyance of his powers." [56] Probably various elements were complicated in the matter, and no one of them can be given the entire preponderance.

No doubt physical sensitiveness or inertia played its part. Gray seems to have been naturally healthy, and if he had lived a healthy life, he might have had little trouble. He was temperate in everything and all his habits were regular. But he was no lover of exercise and the constant use of his brain and very moderate use of his muscles had the customary result. He was rarely ill but never quite well. Something was always hitching and catching in the machinery, with the mental depression naturally consequent. The symptoms are familiar enough: "Less feverish than I was, in a morning: instead of it a sensation of weariness. A soreness in both feet, which goes off in the day, a

frequent dizziness and lightness of head. Easily
fatigued with motion, sometimes a little pain in my
breast, as I had in the winter. These symptoms are
all too slight to make an illness; but they do not
make perfect health." [57] Gray himself could make
sport of them, could trifle with them and turn
them and himself into ridicule: "I have been here
this month or more, low-spirited and full of dis-
agreeablenesses, and to add to them, am at this
present very ill, not with the gout, nor stone (thank
God), nor with blotches, nor blains, nor with frogs
nor with lice, but with a painful infirmity that has
to me the charms of novelty, but would not amuse
you much in the description." [58] Yet it all meant
a constant slight weight upon the spirits, which
the surroundings of Cambridge did not do much
to dissipate.

Also, it meant nerves sensitive to everything,
liable to be oppressed with fears, real or imaginary,
on every occasion and at every opportunity. As so
often happens in such cases, it is not the great fears
that count. Gray would no doubt at any time have
faced the abstract thought or the real presence of
death with as much courage as is possible to frail
mortality; death, that is, apart from "pain, the
only thing that makes death terrible." [59] But he

shrunk and quivered at little dangers and was haunted in his dreams by possible peril that might never come. Especially he dreaded fire, and his sensitiveness on the subject, being well known, perhaps exposed him to more or less legendary pranks from his boisterous college neighbors.[60] The anxiety that haunted him is well depicted in his reference to one case of fire in London: " 'Tis strange that we all of us (here in town) lay ourselves down every night on our funereal pile, ready made, and compose ourselves to rest, while every drunken footman and drowsy old woman has a candle ready to light it before the morning." [61]

On the other hand, it must not be supposed that Gray's superb intelligence could not dominate his nerves. It could and did. There was nothing whatever about him of the abnormal that tainted Cowper, no real obsession, no mad whim or wildly haunting fancy. He was sane, rational, wise, discreet, able to give sage counsel to his friends and, what is so much more difficult, to profit by it himself. Nerves, depression, spiritual dread, all these he thought could be conquered by a mind quietly self-disciplined, and though he did not always maintain such discipline, he knew its nature and could apply it enough to escape serious damage. "A life spent out of the world has its hours of despondence, its inconveniences, its sufferings as numerous and as real (though not quite of the same sort) as a life spent in the midst of it. The power we have, when we will exert it, over our own minds, joined to a little strength and consolation, nay, a little pride we catch from those that seem to love us, is our only support in either of these conditions." [62] By such aid he supported himself with decency and dignity, lived long in his remote, sequestered corner and melted out of the world, apparently, as a man, a perfect bit of alms for the vast erasure of oblivion.

Then the "Elegy" gave him such glory as has fallen to few in the history of literature. The poem was well known and prized in his lifetime, as appears from Wolfe's famous use of it. But who could foresee the immensity of reputation which would enfold its author through the centuries to come? To have written Gray's "Elegy," probably, on the whole, the poem most read and quoted and remembered in the English language, what fullness of fame could any one desire more?

Would it have pleased the quiet Cambridge eremite? Does it please him if he is aware of it? I think so, in spite of his proclamation of the emptiness of glory. When he looks down from his celestial leisure in the brief intervals between endless delicious novels of Marivaux and Crébillon, I think the adoring iteration of millions must be not wholly unacceptable.

IV
HORACE WALPOLE

CHRONOLOGY

Horace Walpole
Born, September 24, 1717
Went to Cambridge, 1735
Abroad, 1739-1741
Entered Parliament, 1741
The Castle of Otranto published, 1764
Gave up Parliament, 1768
Madame du Deffand died, 1780
Became Earl of Orford, 1791
Died, London, March 2, 1797

HORACE WALPOLE

I

During all the last two thirds of the eighteenth century, Horace Walpole held a mirror to the faults and follies and fascinations of the great world. He devoted his time mainly to keeping the mirror bright, polished, and gleaming and to enjoying mirror and reflection both.

Few human beings ever had better opportunities for living such a life. Born in 1717, he stepped almost at once into the atmosphere of kings and courts. His father was a favorite and popular prime minister and a most curious and striking figure. He was a rough English squire who hunted foxes, told dirty stories, laughed, and, by judicious political corruption governed England wisely and peacefully for twenty years. The son took little direct part in politics, had no taste for them, or indeed for any active intervention in the world's affairs. But he moved daily and always among the most prominent people, knew them not only in their state garments and ceremonial manners but in all their fireside and bed-chamber littleness. Royal dukes were trifles to him: his niece married one. Peers were as familiar and as indifferent as other folks. When he was over seventy and tottering toward the grave he became a peer himself. Authors and artists courted and flattered him. Great scholars corresponded with him. And he corresponded with them and with everybody, and made his letters, next to Voltaire's, the most remarkable epitome of a historical epoch that has ever come down to us.

Not that there was any profound philosophical consideration in Walpole's view of things. He made plenty of reflections but they did not go very deep. Nor had he the passionate ardor with which Saint-Simon probed human souls. But all that the most quick and vivid curiosity, watching from the most favorable angle, can do to portray the huge spectacle of the world, Horace Walpole has certainly done.

The great events that stirred the eighteenth century can all be studied in his pages, at least in their English and in their superficial aspects. The Rebellion of 1745, that last desperate effort of the

Stuarts, came close home to him and he shows most
clearly the attitude of a loyal and somewhat terri-
fied adherent of the House of Brunswick. The
vicissitudes of the Seven Years' War are indicated
in the midst of London gossip and the daily doings
of the crowd. The long-drawn agony of the American struggle appears in all its length, and it is to
be noted that Walpole's sympathy was often with
the colonists. Finally, the lurid shadow of the
French Revolution hangs over the closing volumes,
and here, with the conservatism natural to age,
Walpole's hopes and fears were for the members of
his own class and the old order of civilization, which
seemed to him, as to so many others, utterly im-
periled by the wild Gallic frenzy.

Not one of the prominent actors in all these
tumultuous doings fails to make his figure on Walpole's wide and variegated stage. The show personages are there, the popes and emperors, the
kings and queens and princes. They are all handled gayly and with precious little respect, as by
one who knew their human foibles too well. And
attempts to toady to them are made light of, as in
this account of a parson's obituary on a prince:
"He had no great parts . . . but he had great
virtues; indeed, they degenerated into vices: he was

very generous, but I hear his generosity has ruined a great many people; and then his condescension was such, that he kept very bad company." [1] The writer's nearness to royalty is insinuated, though slighted: "How strange are the accidents of life! At ten years old I had set my heart on seeing George I, and . . . I was carried by the late Lady Chesterfield to kiss his hand; . . . and now, fifty years afterwards, one of his great-grandsons and one of his great-granddaughters are my great-nephew and niece." [2] But royalty is a petty thing, not only in the English Georges but in the Louis of France and the rhyming, fighting Fredericks of Prussia and in that curious, murderous, lecherous, fiendishly clever Czarina Catherine who ruled a vast acreage beyond the confines of the civilized world.

Then there are the statesmen, who move these royal puppets, at any rate in civilized England; statesmen who live to serve their country, when they happen to be our own relatives, or mainly to serve their own ambition when they happen to be our relatives' enemies. They are far more interesting than the puppets; yet even they have too often wily tongues and oily hands. And Walpole paints them at full length, every one. There is his own

father, and the son's energy and ingenuity in his
father's defence are always commendable and
usually dignified. But what a world of thoughts
is bred by the elder Walpole's remark, which his
son records: "that but few men should ever be
ministers, for it lets them see too much of the bad-
ness of mankind." [3] There is the great Pitt,
later the great Chatham. It is interesting to see
how Walpole's personal grudge checks and colors
his laudation of the mighty minister. Yet through
the grudge are always to be seen the energy, the
large ambition, the passionate earnestness, the unfailing genius. And there is Fox, all gifts and no
stability. And there is Rockingham, with little
more stability and no gifts. And there is North,
that strangely winning yet fatal spirit, so auspicious
to America, so disastrous to England, whom Walpole gibbets, perhaps justly, as "a bad minister
and a selfish man, who had abilities enough to have
made a very different figure." [4] But a singular
observation on them all, after fifty years' study,
may be taken for what it is worth: "I told her it
was a settled maxim of mine *that no great country
was ever saved by good men,* because good men will
not go the lengths that may be necessary." [5]

Beside the great and serious statesmen there

are the freaks and oddities who diversify solemn moments with whim and antic. A detached spectator like Walpole naturally takes great delight in these, and his picturesque account of them compels the reader to share his amusement. Many of the stories that he tells are trivial and he admits them to be so; but there is shrewd justice in his excuse: "I don't know whether you will not think all these very trifling histories; but for myself, I love anything that marks a character strongly." [6] So the wayward and fantastic figures dance across the stage; those of greater note and importance like the witty and brilliant Charles Townshend, or the social Selwyn with his strangely mortuary tastes, and those less familiar but often more piquant, like Scrope or the Duchess of Kingston. Most singular, most clownish of all, at least, in Walpole's presentation of him, is the ever-reappearing Duke of Newcastle, with his extravagant silliness, his inevitable gesture of colossal ineptitude. Take him crying, capering, cowering at the solemn ceremony of the interment of George the Second in 1760: "This grave scene was fully contrasted by the burlesque Duke of Newcastle. He fell into a fit of crying the moment he came into the chapel, and flung himself back in a stall, the Archbishop

HORACE WALPOLE

hovering over him with a smelling-bottle—but in two minutes his curiosity got the better of his hypocrisy, and he ran about the chapel with his glass to spy who was or was not there, spying with one hand, and mopping his eyes with t'other. Then returned the fear of catching cold, and the Duke of Cumberland, who was sinking with heat, felt himself weighed down, and turning round, found it was the Duke of Newcastle standing upon his train to avoid the chill of the marble." [7]

Such scenes, with or without conspicuous historical figures, are scattered everywhere through Walpole's pages and prove what theatrical delight he took in the vast, disordered show to which he had such intimate access. There are the elaborate trials and executions of the rebel Stuart lords in the beginning; later there are the Gordon riots; there is the superbly picturesque trial of Warren Hastings at the end. And all between there are vivid, telling incidents of every kind; a public wedding or a public hanging, a hot debate in the House of Commons, perhaps an earthquake, which jars the observer as well as the rest of the world, but cannot prevent his getting amusement out of it afterwards, and recording odd occurrences and clever speeches, as that of the parson "who came into White's the

morning of earthquake the first, and heard bets
laid on whether it was an earthquake or the blowing
up of powder-mills, went away exceedingly scan-
dalized, and said, 'I protest, they are such an im-
pious set of people, that I believe if the last trumpet
was to sound, they would bet puppet-show against
Judgment.' " [8]   So, from the eager, hurried jumble
of his crowded days and nights the man drew
an ever-renewed satisfaction for his insatiable
curiosity, and commented on it with a certain
breadth if not depth of historical generalization:
"If I have tired you by this long narrative," he
writes of one singular incident, "you feel differently from me. The man, the manners of the country, the justice of so great and curious a nation, all
to me seem striking, and must, I believe, do more
so to you, who have been absent long enough to
read of your own country as history." [9]

With the historical personages and events there
were the authors and artists. Walpole indeed had
little to do directly with any Bohemian society.
Actual Grub Street would have offended his delicate taste and aristocratic correctness. But constant whiffs of that slovenly, unhandsome world
came betwixt the wind and his nobility, and even
while he held his lordly nose he was careful to set

106

them down. Lady Mary Wortley, to be sure, was
a peeress as well as a writer; but she was dirty as
any Bohemian, and Walpole, who disliked her,
noted her dirt as well as her cleverness. Dr. Johnson was not strictly Bohemian, but he certainly
inhabited Grub Street and, worse still, he was a
Tory and therefore not likely to get Walpole's
good word: "Prejudice, and bigotry, and pride, and
presumption, and arrogance, and pedantry are the
hags that brew his ink, though wages alone supply
him with paper." [10] Actors and singers and
painters also find their place, Garrick and Mrs.
Siddons and Sir Joshua and many another; for
London after all was a small town and there was
not a corner in it that Walpole's eager human instinct could not penetrate.

Yet undoubtedly he was most at home in the
polished, courtly social world into which he was
born; and its sayings and doings, its passions, its
scandals, its diversions, its laughter form the background against which all his painting of larger
things and people necessarily stands out. The love
affairs of all these idle men and women charmed
him, their marrying and giving in marriage, their
running about after pretty faces and mighty fortunes, then squandering the fortunes and crowding

the forgotten, old, worn, pretty faces into the gutter. What a part the two beautiful Gunnings play for him, with their wooers and their triumphs and their mishaps and their fading away! Then there are the diversions of all this noisy, futile, vanishing mob. There is whist, which comes in like a mania and takes possession of society, charming dukes and dowagers and brides and bullies out of their sleep and their money and their wit, if they ever had any. There are the public places of entertainment, Vauxhall and Ranelagh, where everybody goes because everybody else goes, and comes away bored because everybody else was there. And over all the medley of social dainties is sprinkled a sauce of piquant anecdotes, invented or borrowed or begged or stolen, sometimes trivial, sometimes dirty, but almost always amusing and often worthy of a place in memory.

Only, it is the gay world, the wealthy world, the happy, or should-be happy world that makes the substance of all this. The vast foundation of common human labor and need and suffering is singularly absent. When particular cases of misery were called to his notice, Walpole could, no doubt, be sympathetic enough, and he is by no means deficient in general humanity. But the herd,

the million, the grubbers below Grub Street, as
individuals, were left out of his pages because they
were left out of his thoughts. They existed because God had made a queer world. Probably
they served their purpose. Even, if you reflected
upon it, their lot was desperately pitiable and you
wished something might be done for them. Mean-
time you thanked God you were not born one of
them and forgot them, till the French Revolution
most indecently forced them upon your attention,
and then they became a horror.

So, the conclusion was that the way to treat existence was to dissipate your worthless self in the
swift, shifting, flashing, distracting pageant of life
and death. You might not get happiness out of it:
"I have a million of times repented returning to
England, where I never was happy, nor expect to
be." [11] You might feel that your appetite for
excitement and diversion was so endless that even
that wild world could not fill it: "I who love to ride
in the whirlwind, cannot record the yawns of
such an age." [12] Yet yawning in company was
better than yawning alone, and to see and to
hear and to tell some new thing was all that
could make you quite sure that you were out of
the grave.

II

But a man cannot be wholly eyes and ears, or even tongue. There is a stomach to fill, a palate to tickle, a back to warm, nerves that fret and throb and quiver and grow weary, a heart that will sometimes ache if it has not tenderness to satisfy it. As to the material side, it is hardly necessary to say that Walpole was always luxuriously provided for. Through his father's affectionate care he had abundance of money and, while he spent liberally for himself, and to some extent for others, he was shrewd and far-sighted enough to protect himself against financial disaster. His health also was at least such as to enable him to enjoy life. He was always complaining of his own insignificance and frailty; but he took good care of himself and did not suffer abnormally, although the gout was a frequent intruder. He made light of his own practical gifts in all lines; but he probably had more of them than he cared to admit, at any rate so far as his own comfort was concerned.

As to the finer spiritual sides and needs, Walpole certainly recognized them and in his way endeavored to satisfy them. When he wrote, at a period considerably past middle age, "I have a more manly

110

resolution, which is to mend myself as much as I can, and not let my age be as absurd as my youth. I want to respect myself, the person in the world whose approbation I desire most," [13] he was unquestionably sincere. At the same time his natural drift was toward the surface of things and his natural instinct was to play with the deeper thoughts and passions, to shuffle them off and forget them. In other words he was all his life essentially and in the highest degree a dilettante, that is, a person who somehow takes great matters by their petty aspects because he is incapable of taking them in any other way, even with the best will in the world. He looked like a dilettante: little, finical, dainty, airy, insubstantial, and to the day of his death he was one. To be sure he could at times be vehement, make a great apparent fuss about trifles, "a light-headed man, in whose greatest intermissions there is always vehemence enough." [14] But the vehemence, when it was not calculated, was effervescent and did not seriously agitate even the somewhat shallow depths beneath. The saving virtue in it all was that he appreciated his own dilettantism, and did not insist that he was more serious or more lofty than he really was. In this way the dilettantism was compatible with a

certain amount of sincerity, and with a certain good
nature and kindliness which Macaulay, in his rhetorician's impatience, did not enough recognize.
Yet perhaps Macaulay himself was a dilettante
without knowing it.

So you may follow Walpole's dilettantism
through everything. No one will deny that he was
a dilettante statesman. His father's influence and
position took him into Parliament. He attended
regularly for a good many years, and sometimes
spoke. But it cannot be said that he affected the
destinies of England, nor was he desirous to do so.
"I should have made a miserable politician had I
ever felt a sensation of ambition." [15] His own
summary of his political life cannot be improved:
"I go to balls, and to the House of Commons—to
look on; and you will believe me when I tell you,
that I really think the former the more serious
occupation of the two." [16]

He was a dilletante author. His novel "The
Castle of Otranto" set a fashion of mystery stories;
but it is pasteboard, like his own castle and like
himself. His one tragedy was rather horrible than
tragic. His verses were trifles and were meant to
be nothing more. His memoirs are curious, perhaps veracious, yet certainly not profound. But in

authorship, as in other things, he made no claims, and, while he would have disliked to have others say what he said of himself, his modesty must be counted to his credit even if not absolutely sincere. "I wrote early from youth, spirits, and vanity; and from both the last when the first no longer existed. I now shudder when I reflect on my own boldness." [17] Underneath there was always the obscure feeling that authors belong in that horrible Grub Street and never, never would he take up his abode in such a region or have posterity imagine that he did. But what he could write was letters, and he knew it and was proud of it. To be sure they are literary and conscious letters; they do not bare the soul to the extent that Lamb's do, or Flaubert's, or Voltaire's; but then there was little soul to bare and what there was was hardly worth baring. For showing off the great, motley, glittering surface of the world who could beat him? So when he was eighteen years old, an age when surely most men are not preserving their correspondence, he writes anxiously, "You have made me a very unreasonable request, which I will answer with another as extraordinary: you desire I would burn your letters; I desire you would keep mine." [18] For a dilettante author that was beginning young.

The same spirit affects all Walpole's dealings with art and artistic matters. He himself did not paint; but he was a wide and curious connoisseur. His father was a great collector of pictures and there are moments when something like actual passion seems to flicker through Horace's own collecting, as when he writes of a work of Domenichino, "I think I would live upon a flitch of bacon and a bottle of ink, rather than not spare the money to buy it myself." [19] Then we read, "I forgot that I was outbid for Oliver Cromwell's nightcap," [20] and we see what it all means or does not mean.

In rural surroundings and charms Walpole's interest was much less intense and sincere than in the fine arts. He liked what his century called "a noble prospect," especially if it had a temple in it or a rustic bridge or grotto with a few naked nymphs squatting about in verdant umbrage. He liked a pseudo-pastoral background to a pseudo-pastoral festivity. But of solitary rambles in the fields and woods with birds and flowers and thoughts there is not a trace in all his fifteen volumes of letters. "I hate the country," [21] he says frankly. It was simply a place to get away from the city and whet your appetite for going back.

With this idea of the country in mind he made

himself the toy castle of Strawberry Hill, near enough to London to get all the gossip and far enough to get a quiet nap if he needed it. All Walpole's dilettantism was poured out on this dainty little residence. There were bits of Gothic and bits of classic, stained glass and cathedral monuments, altars and fragmentary goddesses, and curiosities like Cromwell's nightcap thrown in for good measure. Royalties and peeresses and foreign beauties came to see it, and the owner showed them about with his apologetic compliment and witty embroidery, and cuddled and petted his dilettante delight in it all, and then wrote to Mann what a bore it was, and generally enjoyed himself to the fullest extent.

As it was an amusement to cultivate the arts with the distinguished ease of a gentleman of quality, so it was diverting to patronize authors and ꞏartists. And Walpole's real kindness must not be forgotten here. He liked to help and did help. If there was some carelessness and more misunderstanding in his treatment of Chatterton, it was certainly not intentional. And he did not really overrate the position and the value of a Mæcenas. "I am not proud of being a favorer of the arts, but it is better than Illustrissimos and Eccellenzas.

. . . Who will throw away a moment's reflection on a dedication to *me?* . . . Yet this is a farthing's worth of fame that many men covet! . . . I laugh at the world, I laugh at myself, and you will laugh at me too for this long monologue." [22] Yet one likes many things that one laughs at. The glory of printing Gray's Odes at Strawberry was worth having, all the same. It was pleasant to be appealed to for a subscription and to give it, pleasant to be asked to speak a good word for a struggling playwright. One did these things, and they much increased one's sense of being far, far above that odious Grub Street.

It was pleasant to make light of scholarship, also, and infinitely easier than to acquire it. Walpole delighted to write dilettante books about art and about history, collected curious anecdotes and bits of gossip, often illustrative and of permanent value. But long days of dusty drudgery in dim libraries with the mice and spiders were not for him. If a pedigree had to be traced, or a legend followed up and exploded, Gray would be glad to do it, or Cole: they liked that sort of thing. And the reputation of being a learned man was the very last that appealed to this butterfly flitter about the bright blossoms of the world. It would be worse even

116

than Grub Street: "Gray says (very justly) that learning never should be encouraged, it only draws out fools from their obscurity; and you know I have always thought a running footman as meritorious a being as a learned man." [23]

On the other hand, there is this to be said for the intellectual attitude of the dilettante: it is compatible with independence, with forming one's own judgment, such as it is, without regard to the pedantry of professors or the dogmatism of the academic mind. Why should a gentleman praise a poem or a picture because he is told to? These things are made for him, not he for them. If they please him, well and good; if not, who cares what they are? Thus Walpole often has an interesting and stimulating freshness of judgment where a deeper thinker might be stuck fast in a rut. If Virgil bores him he says so, and even those whom Virgil does not bore may be grateful to him. [24] His comment on Dante is a little surprising, but after some things one has read one finds it refreshing: "Dante was extravagant, absurd, disgusting— in short, a Methodist parson in Bedlam." [25]

Something the same advantage attends the dilettante in matters of abstract thinking on religion and politics. It would be preposterous to consider

117

Walpole's ideas on such subjects as of serious importance. He would have been the first to smile at such a thing himself. He had a sort of set, fixed opinions when you delved down to them, or rather captured them; for they fluttered high rather than were hidden deep. He wrote Madame du Deffand with solemnity, "I believe firmly in a God, all-powerful, all just, abounding in love and pity." [26] In politics he considered himself a moderate, enlightened Liberal; believed in government for the people, of course by the intelligent class to which he himself belonged; mocked at kings and divine right and aristocratic privilege, till it was seriously threatened. He believed in a comfortable liberty for everyone. Equality would have seemed to him absurd, as it still does to many other good people. But his chief merit in all these views was that he was supremely tolerant about them. He did not take life seriously, or himself seriously. He certainly was not going to take any doctrine or dogma seriously. He liked to quote, if he did not originate, the saying, "this world is a comedy to those who think, a tragedy to those who feel." [27] He did not wish the game of thinking, as he knew it, to be turned into tragic feeling by those who would infuse passion and bitterness and cruelty into the things of men or the things of God.

Walpole's dilettantism is less obvious in social concerns than elsewhere, because the whole social world that he moved in was chiefly governed by a dilettante spirit. It was not a world of real affection or sympathy, or even of a profound human interest, but simply of curiosity and prattle and the haunting, unappeasable desire to escape from oneself. Dancing gave place to cards, and cards to lovemaking, and lovemaking to scandal, the whole seasoned with a perpetual chatter, spiced at times with wit, often clouded and clogged with illimitable boredom. And Walpole danced and chattered through it all, from eight to eighty, really no doubt contributing to the wit, for he had a large fund of cleverness though not a trace of the sweet playfulness of Cowper or the subtle, dissolving humor of Lamb. And he enjoyed it as much as any one could, being apparently built by nature for that sort of thing. Sometimes he yawns behind his hand, sometimes the noise and clatter grow so repellent that he mistakes himself for a misanthrope and really announces a wish to withdraw altogether. "I am so far from growing used to mankind by living amongst them, that my natural ferocity and wildness does but every day grow worse. They tire me, they fatigue me; . . . I fling open the windows, and fancy I want air; and when I get by myself, I undress myself, and seem to have had people in my pockets, in my plaits, and on my shoulders!" [28]

He was young when he wrote this, but it represented a mere passing mood or fancy. He returned to the throng, he could not keep away from it. Old age, of course, meant a decent assumption of repose, gave an excuse for doing only what you wished to do: "I aim at nothing but perfect tranquillity; and am so fortunate, that, if nothing disturbs me, my own temper never does. I carefully avoid everything that can create any disquiet in me." [29] But people and the gay world and the dilettante enjoyment of them were his life, and always continued to be so. "I have been out three times, and today have made five-and-twenty visits, and was let in at six; and, though a little fatigued, am still able, you see, to finish my letter." [30] Not a bad record for a man of seventy-three, who prided himself on delicate health.

Walpole's dilettantism is less manifest where his affections are concerned than anywhere else. It is impossible to deny him a certain large kindliness and sensibility. This appears, at least in words, as regards the more general aspects of suffering in human beings, even in animals: "You know the partiality I have to the afflicted, the disgraced, and the oppressed." [31] And again, "I welcome pain: for it gives me sensibility, and punishes my pride; Donatello loses his grace when I reflect on the million of my fellow creatures that have no one happiness, no one comfort." [32] Such reflections should be credited, even when they do not color a life, or give rise to much accordant deed.

Also, Walpole loved his friends, so far as he was capable of it, and he himself had a fair opinion of his capacity. His mother's memory he adored and we have seen that he was always loyal to that of his father. The rest of his family were not very much to him. But for the two Manns, for Montague, for Chute, for Selwyn he cherished tenderness that even occasionally was realized in self-sacrificing action. He had expressions of fine and delicate feeling: "A death is only to be felt, never to be talked over by those it touches." [33] Have we not all of us known times when we might profit by that? For his cousin Henry Seymour Conway he had a peculiar affection and an admiration perhaps not quite so preposterous as Macaulay deemed it.

121

Yet, after all, his own understanding of his own nature peeps out even in the warmest utterance of this special regard: "If I ever felt much for anything (which I know may be questioned), it was certainly for my mother. I look on you as my nearest relation by her, and I think I can never do enough to show my gratitude and affection to her." [34]

III

One would not expect from a temperament like Walpole's any great display of love in the more erotic sense. Such love is liable to afflict all tempers and at all seasons, even where one looks for it least; but one could hardly be more surprised at it anywhere than here. There is certainly very little trace of love affairs in Walpole's correspondence. He was intimate with hosts of women, laughed with them, gossiped with them, analyzed their foibles and on occasion commended their merits. But even when he was twenty-four he preferred crockery: "For virtù, I have a little to entertain you: it is my sole pleasure—I am neither young enough nor old enough to be in love." [35] As to marriage, the following passage does not display what can be called enthusiasm: "I own, I cannot much felicitate anybody that marries for love. It is bad enough to marry; but to marry where one loves, ten times worse. It is so charming at first, that the decay of inclination renders it infinitely more disagreeable afterwards." [36]

Yet when this gay, superficial, unloving, unloved life had extended to fifty years there came into it the strange, volcanic tenderness of that blind old French woman of seventy, Madame du Deffand. This lady was the opposite of Walpole in nearly every element of character. She was cynical and bitter where he was flippant and diverted. She thought everything false and, far worse, hollow, where he thought everything amusing. In her youth she had lived in a blind whirl of dissipation under the Orleans regency, a whirl which made Walpole's lively surroundings seem like soberness. Yet it is doubtful whether in the gayest madness of it all she found amusement or even oblivion. She had princes to make love to her, poets to sing for her, great wits to laugh with her. In her age she was infirm and blind and, though certainly not deserted, by no means the prominent figure she was in her youth. Yet it does not appear that her dissatisfaction and disgust with life was a matter of circumstances at all; it sprang rather from some deeper source within herself.

At any rate, disgust there was, vast, enduring, and almost suffocating. Lovers were false, friends were indifferent, life meant nothing and led nowhere: "Isn't it strange to meet no one whom one can perfectly esteem? Nothing is so disgusting as life. Ah, I understand all the reasons you have for despising mankind." [37] Worse even than the hatefulness of life was the tediousness and emptiness of it. Of all people who have ever lived, Madame du Deffand seems to have suffered most from ennui; at any rate, no one has described it so elaborately and, it must be said, so interestingly. The long afflicting days, and longer nights, seemed to cover her with a pall and smother her. Could one express negation more effectively than thus? "I hear nothings, I speak nothings, I take interest in nothing, and from nothing to nothing I fare onward to the moment close at hand when I shall become nothing." [38]

Yet when you delve under this surface veil of cynicism and indifference to the deepest depths of this woman's soul, you find a singular nobility, a strange, haunting, searching, yearning tenderness. Like so many passionate pessimists, she was but an idealist upside down, one who asked so much of life, made so many lofty demands upon it that nothing in this mixed and troubled world could ever satisfy her. She went patiently, obscurely seeking for something, and because the something could not be found, the sun lost its lustre and the stars their charm. Here she tells the story, as she does so often: "I do not know why I was fated to grow old: apparently it is so that there might be an individual who had known all the miseries of every age: I know well what was needed to make them all delightful, but it is what I have never found." [39]

It was love she wanted, someone to be devoted to her unselfishly, someone still more to whom she could pour out the rich treasures of her passionate woman's heart. Hear her tell it herself: "Every one loves in his own way: I have only one way of loving, infinitely or not at all." [40] Yet always beside the throbbing heart was the cold, questioning, mistrusting intellect. The final word of her whole life sums it up. She said to her secretary Wiart, when he wept as she was dictating her last letter to Walpole: "You love me then?" And who shall say whether she had loved most or doubted most?

So at seventy she fell in love with Horace Walpole, the fluttering, the mocking, finical, critical Horace Walpole. Was there ever a more singular freak of Eros? And how did Walpole take it? On the whole, not so badly. He was a vain creature, an intensely social creature, and like all such he feared ridicule above all things. What would the mocking wits in Paris and London say to this sentimental, Platonic infatuation of an old woman for his gay, irresponsible, loveless maturity? So he tried all he could to restrain her ardors, laughed at her a little, petted her a little, sympathized when it was absolutely necessary. The situation really was trying and the indefatigable letter writer, who wanted all his correspondence saved for posterity, urged and begged that his letters to this over-zealous friend might be destroyed, partly because he knew they were in bad French and partly because he feared that they were foolish. Yet with it all he was fond of Madame du Deffand, treated her and speaks of her with a tenderness unusual for him, and evidently felt obscurely that in his frivolous and artificial life such a blaze of real passion was too rare and precious a thing to be altogether rejected or neglected.

But what she felt about him is a far more curious

126

study. Her judgment of him is profoundly helpful, for she was one of the most acute observers of the soul that ever lived, where her own passions were not concerned. When she read him calmly, she saw his weaknesses and noted them. His vanity as to his letters? How childish it is: "Nothing is more annoying than your eternal excuses about the insipidity of your letters. Why should they be insipid? Can the letters of a friend be so?" [41] Ridicule? Why fear it? Why bother about it? Be yourself, be sincere and let the ridicule go: "You fear mortally being found fault with, and above all, being ridiculous." [42] Yet in spite of these rare moments of insight, generally she sees him with the coloring, magnifying glasses of her devoted affection and he appears to her a superior being. Horace Walpole! Fancy! She admires his gift of contentment: "You are happier than others, you can go without things, you know how to be alone, you are sufficient to yourself, and I, I have no desire but to escape myself at all times." [43] She praises his common sense, his insight, his knowledge of the world, his knowledge of his own heart. She compares him to Henri Quatre, which would seem to be startling enough: "He was equal to you in good sense and in common sense, but you

have a gentler soul." [44]   Then she goes further
still, and compares him to God, to be sure with a
slight touch of sarcasm: "You have a thousand
points of resemblance to the Divinity, but particularly that with both one never knows whether one
is esteemed worthy to be loved or hated." [45]
It will probably be admitted that any one who
could make a deity out of Horace Walpole must
be very far gone. What would Gray have thought
of it?

The poor lady *was* far gone. No schoolgirl of
sixteen could have cherished an infatuation more
complete. She asks his advice, wants him to guide
and counsel her out of his exhaustless wisdom and
experience, as indeed, for all her acuteness, she
was always anxious for advice and help. She is
afraid of offending him, of boring him, with the
ardor and tenderness of her letters: "I must learn
to walk upon eggs, for what I fear most in the
world is giving you the slightest occasion to scold
me." [46]   And he does scold her and she resents
it, cannot understand his coldness and indifference.
Is love like hers such a cheap commodity that he
can afford to throw it away? "The letter that I
have just received is so offensive and I should say,
if I dared, so extravagant, that I should throw it

into the fire without an answer." [47] *Should,* she
says, you will notice, not *shall.* There are times
when she is driven to the despairing resolution of
breaking off altogether: "You write me," she says,
"that I desire only to make slaves, that I love only
myself, and that as you also love only yourself, we
can never agree. Very well, sir, let us disagree,
and let us end a correspondence which for you has
long been nothing but a persecution." [48] But
how could such a love break off? And in one of
the very last letters she writes before her death in
1780 is this charming phrase: "You will regret me,
because it is a beautiful thing to know that one
has been loved." [49]

So the dilettante was profoundly and strangely
worshiped. Then, as the years slipped by and
Time's whirligig brought in his customary re-
venges, the dilettante came to worship in his turn.
When he himself was seventy years old, as Madame
du Deffand had been at the beginning of her attachment, he met the two Miss Berrys, Mary and
Agnes. Immediately his thoughts and interests
became centred upon them, as the French lady's
had been upon him, except that Walpole's affection
was hardly capable of her wild ardors and immense
despairs. But the girls were charming, and the gay

old merrymaker of Strawberry Hill was completely
charmed by them. In fact, if it was a question of
ridicule, he was much more exposed to it in this
affair than in the earlier one. Not, it must be said,
that he made himself really ridiculous. He was
too intelligent and too widely experienced in the
world to do anything that the world would brand
as senile, or even as quite undignified. "If you
were really my wives, I could not be more generally applied to for accounts of you; of which I am
proud. I should be ashamed if, at my age, it were
a ridiculous attachment." [50]

But it all gave a singular grace and color to the
fading years. Love had always seemed a toy, a
trifle, like all the other serious interests of life. It
was no better now; but in its way it was exquisite,
and during the few remaining days you might as
well make the most of it. So he chatted with his
"two wives," as he called them, counseled them,
planned for them, was anxious as to their happiness, as to their health, as to their friends, as to
their abodes. Above all, such being especially his
nature, he wrote them infinite letters, full of
piquant anecdotes, of highly-spiced and brilliant
memories, full also of those touches of tenderness
which Madame du Deffand long before had lav-

ished upon him. "I do pique myself on not being ridiculous at this very late period of my life; but when there is not a grain of passion in my affection for you two, . . . I am not ashamed to say that your loss is heavy to me. . . . Adieu, my dearest friends: it would be tautology to subscribe a name to a letter, every line of which would suit no other man in the world but the writer." [51]   Elsewhere he signed himself "Horace Fondlewives." [52] What would Madame du Deffand have thought? And, since he could not well marry both, it is said that he at least offered to marry one, simply that she might have the benefit of his late acquired title and be Countess of Orford after him. She had the good sense to refuse. But is it not curious to see the great dilettante of a dilettante century going out of existence with a dilettante love affair?

It cannot be denied that there is something to be said for Horace Walpole's spiritual attitude. The spectacle of the moving world is inexhaustible in interest and diversion, an endless comedy for those who take it from the thinker's angle. Perhaps the best chance of being happy, or of avoiding unhappiness, is to lose oneself in it. Yet it is a damnable reflection upon life, personal life, your life and my life, that the best thing to do with it is to forget it.

And there is something to be said also for living with intense personal passion, to achieve success, to achieve glory, to help others, to make the world better. Such a passion is full of disappointment and failure and bitterness. It means tired limbs and nerves and sleepless nights. Others disregard our efforts and we ourselves despair over them. Yet if we were made for any purpose, it seems as if we were made to live really. Persons of Walpole's type trifle away existence and do not live at all.

V
WILLIAM COWPER

CHRONOLOGY

William Cowper
Born, Great Berkhamstead, Hertfordshire, November 26, 1731
First derangement, 1752
Attempted suicide because of House of Lords clerkship, 1763
Settled with Unwins in Huntingdon, 1765
Mr. Unwin died, 1767
Removed with Mrs. Unwin to Olney, 1767
The Task published, 1785
Removed to Weston, 1786
Translation of Homer published, 1791
Mrs. Unwin died, 1796
Died, Dereham, April 25, 1800

WILLIAM COWPER *

I

How strange for a man to go through a great part of his life with the absolute conviction that he was unalterably condemned to hell. Yet this was the case of Cowper. Born in 1731 of an old and aristocratic family but with no great means, Cowper began his career, after an excellent education, by failing in the law. As a youth he had some fairly gay acquaintances and experiences. But he soon settled down unmarried to a quiet country life, with plenty of religion, plenty of melancholy, a sprinkling of actual madness, the devotion of women (especially one woman, Mrs. Unwin), constant letter writing by which his later history is well known to us, more or less assiduous authorship and, always, till he died in 1800—hell.

Hell must be the basis of the psychological study of him. And to begin with one asks how he arrived

---

* The name was pronounced "Cooper" by the poet himself. See Wright's edition of Cowper's Correspondence, vol. I, p. xiv.

at the belief in its imminence. The convergence of
natural causes is easy to understand. First, religion in its intensest form hovered over him from
childhood. It was not always a misery. When he
was a small boy at school and was tormented by
one of his elders, the sense of God as a refuge was
his greatest comfort.[1] But comfort was not the
main feature. When he was a trifle older and was
crossing a cemetery at night, he passed a grave-
digger who threw up a skull and struck him.[2]
The incident impressed him deeply, and skulls were
hitting him from somewhere all his life. For a brief
period the distractions of the world helped him to
forget. But in his later remoteness he had religion
about him to the point of suffocation. Not that the
special Calvinistic doctrines of election caused his
trouble. He was a loyal member of the Church of
England and his general views were not intolerably
narrow. His personal damnation was quite peculiar to himself, and the rest of mankind might find
mercy if they deserved it, or sought it. But he ate,
slept, thought, and lived with religion as a background. Prayers, sermons, and spiritual songs
daily enveloped him. Parsons and saints were his
companions and correspondents. They tried to
cheer him by emphasizing the infinite joy of

heaven; but their well meant efforts greatly enhanced the poignancy of hell.

The burden of this external atmosphere was
splendidly seconded by the man's physical constitution. His organic health seems to have been
good enough, nor does he often complain of it.
With proper surroundings and occupations it
might have served him well. But he inherited sensitive nerves, and his habits of thought and life
fostered the sensitiveness in every possible way. He
analyzes it subtly and closely, as he does everything; portraying, for instance, in keen and vivid
words the disastrous effect of intellectual effort:
"The meshes of that fine network, the brain, are
composed of such mere spinner's threads in me,
that when a long thought finds its way into them,
it buzzes, and twangs, and bustles about at such a
rate as seems to threaten the whole contexture." [3]
Hell has a superb chance in persons subject to such
physical states as Cowper delineates in the following passage: "If I do nothing, I am dejected; if I
do anything, I am weary; and that weariness is
best described by the word lassitude, which is of
all weariness in the world the most oppressive." [4]
When to such a natural physical predisposition
you add the eighteenth-century habit of taking

laudanum at any convenient opportunity, you get a state which in the abstract would not be likely to conduce to cheerfulness.

How sensitive Cowper's nerves were and how they tore him to pieces is best shown by his chief attempt to succeed in practical life. The office of Clerk of the Journals of the House of Lords was offered him through the kindness of a relative. But unfortunately it was necessary to appear before the Bar of the House and be examined. To his shy and diffident temper the horror of such publicity was unbearable. He brooded over the matter till it became a nightmare of distressing proportions. Finally there seemed no way to escape but suicide. And for days he struggled to bring himself to this consummation by poison, by drowning, by the knife, and by the cord. But the garter with which he had actually hanged himself broke in time to save his life. After this the Clerkship of the Journals was abandoned.

With such a background of nerves it does not require a psychoanalyst to anticipate any development of melancholy. Cowper himself constantly recognizes his tendency to such a condition: "It pleased God that I should be born in a country where melancholy is the national characteristic;

and of a house more than commonly subject to it. To say truth, I have often wished myself a Frenchman." [5] Even without the shadow of hell, the mere shadow of a dark day or of a petty annoyance was apt to make life seem not worth living. And in a constitution so delicately balanced any unusual strain was always likely to turn the melancholy into actual derangement. This happened in Cowper's case. The full details of the madness are not revealed to us; but it was evidently blighting and horrible enough. The constant threat of it must be always taken into account in studying him.

Combined with this extreme sensitiveness and susceptibility there was in Cowper another element which tended strongly to encourage the fixity of his delusion. He was a man of remarkable confidence in his own opinions and judgment in everything. To be sure he admired Christian humility, commended it in others, and prayed for it himself, confessedly with the distinct consciousness that he needed it. But his natural bent was to vigorous and decided conclusions. He reasoned forcibly, and when he had reasoned it was difficult to change him. Take one small point. He prided himself on his judgment of character by faces, and thought he was not apt to be mistaken. I have usually felt that those who adopted this attitude were misled most easily. Again, Cowper's dogmatic turn showed in a disposition to think himself unique, not only as to hell but as to other things. When a certain kindness was proposed to him, he wrote: "I am, perhaps, the only man living who would hesitate a moment, whether, on such easy terms, he should or should not accept it. But if he finds another like me, he will make a greater discovery than even that which he has already made of the principles of this wonderful art." [6]

It is now easier to understand how such a combination of circumstances could facilitate the belief which made a horror of all Cowper's later years. He was convinced that God had not only abandoned him, forgotten him, but had made him a special object of punishment and vengeance. For other men there might be salvation and redemption, for him none, but only the wide gaping terror of eternal and inevitable hell. It is difficult to exaggerate the bare vividness with which Cowper conveys and expatiates upon the misery of his situation. In the midst of pleasure he is wretched, in the midst of love he is hated, in the midst of life he is dead and buried. "I lived in Olney once, but now I am buried in it, and have no business with the world on the outside of my sepulchre; my appearance would startle them, and theirs would be shocking to me." [7] The ghastly lyric on his own mind sums up the situation in verse better than any prose could do it:

> Man disavows, and Deity disowns me,
> Hell might afford my miseries a shelter;
> Therefore, hell keeps her ever-hungry mouths all
> Bolted against me. [8]

If we try to trace the causes of the condemnation as Cowper saw them, he makes them comparatively clear to us, however inadequate. He believed that in neglecting to improve the mercies of God on a certain occasion in his early life he had sinned against the Holy Ghost. [9] This was the unpardonable sin and there was no forgiveness and no recovery. His youth had been sinful in many respects, though it does not appear that he ever did anything that the ordinary man would consider even a peccadillo. But after this fatal rejection his doom was fixed. The final judgment was revealed to him in a dream in the year 1773, when he was forty-two years old, [10] and ever after he referred to his fate in the phrase *actum est de te, periisti,* the verdict is passed, thou hast perished.

There were indeed occasional gleams of hope. Prayer, too often denied him as a consolation, sometimes opened a door of comfort. On a sunny day in spring, perhaps, when the south wind was blowing, it might seem impossible that hell should be so near. Then the clouds settled down and the darkness was thicker than ever.

It was the nocturnal voices that did most. In the daytime and the dear light you could seem to live. But in the lonely dark came those dreadful voices, always so symptomatic of madness, and there was no escape from the black terror of them. You were shaken with frightful dreams, and the voices murmured through them *actum est de te, periisti.* You awoke, yes, you knew you were awake, and the voices were only louder and firmer and infinitely more terrible. Laudanum could not quiet them, though who could blame you for taking it? Love could not quiet them. Your best friends argued with you. Their intentions were good. Their arguments were excellent, no doubt. They might have applied to any one else. But no argument made any difference to you: you knew. It was that same old dogmatic positiveness of temperament. The man was gentle about it, polite about it. But nothing could shake him. He was

damned, peculiarly damned, uniquely damned.
And so subtle, so colossal is human egotism that
you see that the pleasure of the uniqueness actually
alleviates even damnation. "I recapitulated in the
most impassioned accent and manner the unex-
ampled severity of God's dealings with me in the
course of the last twenty years, especially in the
year '73, and again in '86, and concluded all with
observing that I *must* infallibly perish, and that the
Scriptures which speak of the insufficiency of man
to save himself can never be understood *unless* I
perish." [11] Sweet solace, to feel that the eternal
loss of your soul is necessary to prove the infalli-
bility of Scripture.

In a life so lived, and with the presence of such
a tormenting terror, it is interesting and curious to
see the part played by suicide. When Cowper was
eleven years old his father, a minister, mind you,
handed him a treatise advocating self-destruction,
and asked his opinion on it.[12] The boy gave it,
positively no doubt, whatever it was, and the father
making no comment, the son interpreted this as
favoring the conclusions of the treatise. It was a
choicely paternal action. How far it influenced
the later Cowper we cannot tell. But suicide was
often in his thoughts, and never very far from his

actual experience. He attempted it over and over again, always realizing perfectly the absurd contradiction of his attitude since he was only bringing himself nearer to the very end he dreaded. Yet human nature is full of such inconsistency, and Cowper was like others, though he hated to think so. How could you paint the inconsistency more vividly than he does when walking along a precipice? "I passed sometimes within a foot of the edge of it, from which to have fallen would probably have been to be dashed to pieces. But though to have been dashed in pieces would perhaps have been best for me, I shrunk from the precipice, and am waiting to be dashed in pieces by other means." [13]

He waited till the natural end. But nothing ever shook his conviction. When he was dying a friend ventured to point out to him that "a merciful Redeemer had prepared unspeakable happiness for all his children—and therefore for him." But Cowper energetically put aside the argument and begged his friend to desist.[14] Up to the very last he preferred being damned to being convinced.

II

It might be supposed that when a man's whole existence was set and framed in such a delusion as

this, he could be only an object of repulsion and
pity, and would be much better forgotten. On
the contrary, Cowper is charming to live with, full
of instruction and diversion, of good counsel and
varied entertainment. In spite of the nerves there
was much of sunshine in his natural temper, and
before the fatal dream had blasted him he could
write of himself: "As to my own personal condition, I am much happier than the day is long, and
sunshine and candlelight see me perfectly contented." [15] All his life he could turn from hell
to all sorts of trifles, play with them, laugh at
them, be busy with them. Even, the same intensity
which made hell take hold of him made the trifles
take hold of him while they were present. "I never
received a *little* pleasure from anything in my life;
if I am delighted, it is in the extreme." To which
he adds characteristically: "The unhappy consequence of this temperature is, that my attachment
to any occupation seldom outlives the novelty of
it." [16] He liked jest and laughter, liked pure
nonsense and had an exquisitely gracious gift at it.
Often his touch in this respect suggests that of.
Lamb. The difference is that with Lamb the jesting instinct was beautifully and subtly infused
through all the tragic background of life. With

Cowper it was merely imposed upon it. I find
the following sentence from Jeremy Taylor quoted
at the end of one of the old lives of Cowper. Taylor
speaks of horrible sounds in general, and adds:
"The groans of a man in a fit of the stone are worse
than all these; and the distractions of a troubled
conscience are worse than those groans; and yet a
careless merry sinner is worse than all that." [17]
You can imagine how heartily Cowper would have
approved the remark—and how Lamb would have
delighted in it.

Cowper, then, dodged hell in every sort of a
mild and sinless diversion. He was always fond of
exercise in the open air. In his youth he indulged
in amusements which would have appeared sinful to
his age. He speaks of dancing all night and shoot-
ing half the day.[18] In his very latest years he
looks back with pleasure to swimming in the
Bay of Weymouth.[19] The death of the fox
would have made hunting distasteful to him, even
if he had been a rider, and his vivid account of the
termination of a hunt is strongly tinged with sarcasm.[20] But walking was at all times his resource and joy. Alone or with a companion he
wandered through the woods and fields, and found

that the activity of the brain was best soothed and banished by the activity of the legs.

Also, when he walked he used his ears and eyes, and external nature was the greatest consoler he could possibly find. It is true that from the standpoint of eternity—and hell—the sun and moon were trifles like other things: "rested in, and viewed without a reference to their Author, what is the earth—what are the planets—what is the sun itself but a bauble?" [21] But they were such delicious trifles! Rarely has the sense of ecstasy in natural objects been expressed with more passion than by this half-mad dreamer: "Oh, I could spend whole days and moonlight nights in feeding upon a lovely prospect. My eyes drink the rivers as they flow." [22]

Nor was it the more unusual or violent aspects of natural beauty that Cowper longed for and appreciated. He did not require mountains or glaciers, strange tropical luxuriance or arctic splendor. Even, in later years at least, a wild outlook oppressed him. Mountains and forests were gloomy and increased his natural melancholy. Just the quiet walks around Weston and Olney were enough.[23] A sunset, the morning star, the drift of clouds in autumn, the wayward notes of birds in woodland silence, he asked no more than these. And his gift for rendering these natural impressions was admirable. To be sure, the closing eighteenth century still kept its hold on him at times, as when, with Johnsonian pompousness, he could talk about "The obsolete prolixity of shade." But when he forgot his literary manners and said what he felt, the result was exquisite. It might be in the prose of the letters: "Here is no noise *save* (as the poets always express it) that of the birds hopping on their perches and playing with their wires, while the sun glimmering through the elm opposite the window falls on my desk with all the softness of moonshine. There is not a cloud in the sky, nor a leaf that moves, so that over and above the enjoyment of the purest calm, I feel a well-warranted expectation that such as the day is, it will be to its end." [24] Or it might be even more perfectly in verse, as in the primrose passage in "The Task," [25] or the summary of nature as it appears in association and recollection:

> "Scenes that soothed
> Or charmed me young, no longer young, I find
> Still soothing and of power to charm me still." [26]

And as Cowper loved wild nature, so he loved it cultivated, loved to keep a garden and work in it, loved a greenhouse also, to plant and transplant and prune and train and finally to enjoy. How little one connects hell with the tranquil delight which saturates the following: "But now I sit with all the windows and the door wide open, and am regaled with the scent of every flower in a garden as full of flowers as I have known how to make it. We keep no bees, but if I lived in a hive I should hardly hear more of their music. All the bees in the neighborhood resort to a bed of mignonette, opposite to the window, and pay me for the honey they get out of it by a hum, which though rather monotonous, is as agreeable to my ear as the whistling of my linnets." [27] All the mechanical occupations implied in country life were acceptable. He liked not only gardening, but carpentering, would wield a hammer and chisel and saw and make pretty odds and ends of all kinds to please himself and help his housemates. Busy fingers teased him out of thoughts quite as well as busy feet.

Then there were pets. All his life Cowper loved animals. When he was being carried off to a mad-house, his last normal interest was that his cat

should be tenderly taken care of.[28] His own state
of hopeless reprobation seemed somehow to throw
him down to the level of the animals, at least
to destroy the super-animal part of him. As he
himself expresses it, with singular quick pathos,
"The season has been most unfavorable to animal
life; and I, who am merely animal, have suffered
much by it." [29] Any one who knows anything of
Cowper at all, knows the charming elaborate
description of his hares, of their lives and deaths,
and the profound interest he took in them. His
birds meant quite as much to him, and the dog,
Beau, the companion of his walks.

In human beings generally and human affairs
Cowper took almost as much interest as in birds
and rabbits. He indeed affected to regard politics
and the movement of the world as quite remote
from him. He was "an extra-mundane character"
and, "though not a native of the moon," "not
made of the dust of this planet." [30] But it would
have been impossible for his dogmatic temper
not to have pronounced judgment on all the doings
of kings and ministers and peoples. The Americans and their Revolution? "If perfidy, treachery,
avarice, and ambition can prove their cause to have
been a rotten one, those proofs are found upon

them." [31] The truth is, he himself was going to the devil and he would have been hardly human if he had not sometimes thought the whole world was tending obscurely in the same direction. He did. Rulers were bad and people were worse, and if England was piping and dancing and rotting herself to final disaster, she had richly deserved it. But the consolation, if it was a consolation, was in the divine management of it all: "The unmanageable prince and the no less unmanageable multitude, have each a mouth into which God can thrust a curb when he pleases, and kings shall reign and the people obey to the last moment of His appointment." [32]

Cowper's interest in the more common concerns of life, as it went on immediately about him, was a much more personal matter. He entered quickly into the peculiarities of the people whom he met, even in a casual fashion, and he had a remarkable faculty of setting off those peculiarities, not harshly or bitterly, but with a singular grace of comic touch. Trifle for trifle, the human trifles were the pleasantest. The classic example of this is the admirable narrative of Gilpin. But the letters have many incidents and characters almost equally delightful, for instance the whirlwind passage of the

Parliamentary candidate through Cowper's quiet household.[33] Again, how vivid is the account of the servingman William and the problem of the lamp: "Now there are certain things which great geniuses miss, and which men born without any understanding at all hit immediately. In justification of the truth of this remark, William, who is a lump of dough, who never can be more dead than he is till he has been buried a month, explained it to *me* in a moment; accordingly we have used it twice, to my great satisfaction." [34]

Nor was Cowper less sensitive to the tragedies of life than to its comic side. Misery touched him, want appealed to him, not only passively but actively. His means were always limited. Indeed, he himself was largely dependent upon the assistance of others, and it required the greatest prudence and frugality to keep expenses within proper bounds. Yet his charity was incorrigible, so much so that his friends complained of it and thought he was perpetually duped. He insisted that he was not, calling to his aid that unfailing insight into character through physiognomy of which he was so proud. At any rate he had at all times a crowd of dependents about him who enjoyed his moderate bounty and showed probably as much gratitude as is usual.

In closer contact with his equals Cowper was not very responsive. At least the grave temper of his mind resented the ordinary frivolity of the world. In his early days he seems to have known what gayety was: balls, routs, games, diversions, chatter. But even then he was apt to shrink from such things and was essentially a shy and solitary mortal. "Visits," he says, "are insatiable devourers of time, and fit only for those who if they did not that, would do nothing." [35] He complains again and again of his extreme shyness: "I am a shy animal, and want much kindness to make me easy. Such I shall be to my dying day." [36]

Yet with the friends whom he loved he could overcome the shyness and reserve, could abound in spirits and light merriment. Over a good dinner of fish or game, such as was so often sent him, he could no doubt play the merry and amiable host.

And especially he liked to pour out his soul to his friends in letters. He had a long list of correspondents, Newton, Unwin, Bull, Hill, later Johnson and Hayley, and always innumerable ladies. I cannot help suspecting that he had a lurking idea that some day the letters would be printed. At any rate, he evidently takes great interest in letter writing as an art, and makes many and charming comments on it. "Puzzle not yourself about a subject when you write to either of us; everything is subject enough from those we love." [37] Indeed everything was a subject for him, and everything he touched was transfigured by wisdom or grace, by pathos or gayety, always with just the little relish of waiting hell to give it a spice.

III

Besides the external trifles which could divert the gaze for a moment from inevitable perdition—sunshine, flowers, birds, animals, kings, treacherous Americans, and men and women—there were internal, spiritual trifles also; trifles of art, trifles of thought, trifles of literary workmanship.

Art might seem far enough from Cowper, and so it was. Yet those busy fingers liked at times to play with the pencil and brush and produce bits of plastic beauty on which he could at any rate rally himself. Music came nearer home. Its infinite spiritual suggestion appealed to Cowper's sensitive nerves. The constant singing of hymns, which to many of us seems a rather desperate form

154

of amusement, was to him soothing, at any rate
compared with some other things. He appears always to have been deeply affected by sound, wit-
ness not only the well-known passage in "The
Task," [38] but the wonderful page in the letter to
Newton, which ends so characteristically: "There
is somewhere in infinite space a world that does
not roll within the precincts of mercy, and as it is
reasonable, and even scriptural, to suppose that
there is music in heaven, in those dismal regions
perhaps the reverse of it is found; tones so dismal, as to make woe itself more insupportable,
and to acuminate even despair." [39] But the most
curious passage, musically, in all Cowper, is the
one in which he at once recognizes the subtle, in-
sinuating charm, and deprecates it with all the
Puritanic passion of his nature and training: "The
lawfulness of it, when used with moderation, and in
its proper place, is unquestionable; but I believe
that wine itself, though a man be guilty of habitual
intoxication, does not more debauch and befool the
natural understanding, than music, always music,
music in season and out of season, weakens and
destroys the spiritual discernment. If it is not used
with an unfeigned reference to the worship of God,
and with a design to assist the soul in the per-

formance of it, which cannot be the case when it is the only occupation, it degenerates into a sensual delight, and becomes a most powerful advocate for the admission of other pleasures, grosser perhaps in degree, but in their kind the same." [40]

Reading was another resource; but, especially in later years, reading was difficult and dangerous; it was too apt to involve or suggest or imply strange matters and lead one into worlds that were far better let alone, if one could. As for thinking, hard thinking, abstract thinking, that was impossible for a brain so torn and worn with inevitable thought. Quick, light, pregnant suggestions you might get if you wanted them. "But thus it is with my thoughts:—when you shake a crab-tree the fruit falls; good for nothing indeed when you have got it, but still the best that could be expected from a crab-tree." [41] Long, exact speculation he could not get. The man loved it but it was death to him. Yet he could divert himself with books delightfully. How he would have enjoyed novels, if they had not seemed to him worse than music! But he could read books of travel and he did; wide wanderings in strange countries, bewildering adventures and fantastic daring which made him hug his quiet fireside all the more closely. Perhaps it was good training for one who was fated to have wilder adventures in the great unknown.

Also, he liked to read the poets, or had done so in his youth, and he had definite opinions about them, expressed with all his usual dogmatism. But in later life he had few such books and read them little, for a rather astonishing reason: "Poetry, English poetry, I never touch, being pretty much addicted to the writing of it, and knowing that much intercourse with those gentlemen betrays us unavoidably into a habit of imitation, which I hate and despise most cordially." [42] He had not perhaps quite grasped the fact that the best recipe for avoiding imitation, next to having read nothing whatever, is the widest reading possible.

But, reading or no reading, he was a poet himself, and poetry was, on the whole, the best of all the numerous trifles that distracted him from hell. He did not take to it extensively till somewhat late in life, but when he did, he took to it wholesale and wrote verses of all sorts. Short or long, grave or gay, instructive or diverting, all was one to him. He could make a comic epic of the story of Gilpin, or he could spend long years in translating the Iliad and Odyssey. Nonsense spattered from his pen as freely as ink, and when the sexton of the parish wanted mortuary verses for his death list, inspiration came quite as readily, but no more so.

The motives that induced him to write were as various as the subjects. If a lady suggested that he should make a poem about a sofa, he would spin it into six books of Miltonic longitude. But though the whims of ladies might be the provoking cause, the fundamental purpose, or so he insisted, was to make the world better. Poets in general were poor creatures: their only serious excuse for being was to moralize, and he moralized, sugaring the pill with primroses and bird songs and other agreeable dainties. And all the time underneath the deepest motive was distraction, to get rid of hell. He himself admits it: "The quieting and composing effect of it was such, and so totally absorbed have I sometimes been in my rhyming occupation, that neither the past nor the future (those themes which to me are so fruitful in regret at other times), had any longer a share in my contemplation." [43] Yet nonsense and mortuary verses both sometimes failed to achieve the end: "Strange as it may seem, the most ludicrous lines I ever wrote have been written in the saddest mood, and, but for that saddest mood, perhaps had never been written." [44]

Whatever the motive, if a man like Cowper set out to write at all, it was certain that he would do his very best. Conscience and thoroughness were characteristic of him, even in trifles. He worked steadily, persistently, and faithfully. That is to say, there were times when he could not work at all, when the mood was unfavorable or external cares and perplexities distracted him too greatly. But he kept his set task before him and returned to it whenever he could catch an hour or a minute. Interruptions, not directly pertinent, were disregarded, and he was willing to write in surroundings which many authors would consider prohibitive.[45]

Also, he not only worked persistently but worked carefully. His first draught was generally turned off with ease, but he revised and criticized his own productions with peculiar zeal and let nothing go that was not as perfect as he could make it. "I am a severer critic upon myself than you would imagine." [46] Again, "Whatever faults, however, I may be chargeable with as a poet, I cannot accuse myself of negligence. I never suffer a line to pass till I have made it as good as I can." [47] Even in the last wretched years, when every hour had its torment, the close and scrupulous revision

of his Homer afforded as much relief as anything:
"I give all my miserable days to the revisal of
Homer, and often many hours of the night to
the same hopeless employment." [48] Hopeless, because back of all the dainty trifles was that yawning gulf, and you could not fill it or hide it, even
with songs and flowers.

And if work would not fill it, assuredly it could
not be filled with anything so insubstantial as glory.
Cowper often expresses the conventional indifference to fame, the vulgar breath of the unthinking
crowd, and all the rest of it. "You tell me that I
am rivaled by Mrs. Bellamy; and he, that I have
a competitor for fame, not less formidable, in the
Learned Pig. Alas, what is an author's popularity
worth, in a world that can suffer a prostitute on
one side and a pig on the other, to eclipse his brightest glories?" [49] Yet criticism annoys him: the
critics are so dull, they seize the wrong end of
things, always praise where they should blame, and
overlook the point on which an author most prides
himself. Moreover, there is an agreeable titillation
in the thought that one's humble verses may reach
the eyes of Majesty itself.[50] In fact, when the
poet speaks out frankly he admits as much desire
of success as might infect a more worldly man: "I

am not ashamed to confess, that having commenced an author, I am most abundantly desirous to succeed as such. I have (what, perhaps, you little suspect me of) in my nature an infinite share of ambition." [51] Yet how strange it is to watch the interplay of this perfectly normal and human instinct with the one appalling dread: "As to fame, and honor, and glory, that may be acquired by poetical feats of any sort, God knows, that if I could lay me down in my grave with hope at my side, or sit with hope at my side in a dungeon all the residue of my days, I would cheerfully waive them all." [52]

IV

So the flavor of hell runs through the whole portrayal of Cowper, necessarily. But what brings it out with the greatest vividness is to see him in his usual surroundings, the infinite peace and domesticity of a conventional English parlor and fireside. If he had lived an earthly life of furious movement, it would not only have helped him to forget, but the transition to the plagues of Hades would have been more agreeably and gradually prepared. Not he. He never moved, hated movement. He did not visit London for years, did not stir from the monotonous tranquillity of his rural environment. His timorous, fluttering spirit could achieve the semblance of serenity only within the mild radiance of the evening lamp, with the click of knitting needles about him and the soothing, inconsequential chatter of women's tongues. The world ran on for him in an even, unbroken course, as if it were to run on so forever. He liked comfort—did not require luxury—liked ordinary domestic comfort, and got it. "On the whole, I believe, I am situated exactly as I should wish to be, were my situation to be determined on by my own election; and am denied no comfort that is compatible with the total absence of the chief of all." [53] His poetry is largely the poetry of home life and humble, simple contentment. That is what gave it such charm for Sainte-Beuve. Perhaps if the French critic had known the atmosphere better he would not have praised it quite so much.[54]

But indeed Cowper was domestic by temperament. He felt the family affections deeply, all of them, and this tenderness is manifest in his letters to the end. With the strange, subtle power of cool analysis, which never deserted him, he dissected his emotions on meeting a dear relative, Lady Hesketh, one of his most cherished friends and correspond-

ents, after a prolonged absence: "Wherefore is it
. . . that together with all those delightful sensa-
tions, to which the sight of a long absent dear
friend gives birth, there is a mixture of something
painful; flutterings and tumults, and I know not
what accompaniments of our pleasure that are in
fact perfectly foreign from the occasion?" [55]   But
however he dissected them, he felt them, and
they were mainly emotions of delight.   As for the
fondness which he cherished for the memory of his
mother, it seems to have been something intimate
and peculiar, and it clung to him in his worst dis-
tresses though it could not banish them.   Probably his best known poem is that on receiving his
mother's picture; but the singular depth of his feeling also finds expression in his letters: "You may
remember with pleasure, while you live, a blessing
vouchsafed to you so long; and I, while I live, must
regret a comfort of which I was deprived so early.
I can truly say, that not a week passes (perhaps
I might with equal veracity say a day), in which
I do not think of her.   Such was the impression
her tenderness made upon me, though the opportunity she had for showing it was so short." [56]
And this was when he was over fifty and his mother
had been dead forty-seven years!

In general, Cowper had a fondness for women
and an attraction for them. He much preferred
substantial domestic qualities to social graces. Although he had danced in his youth, he thought you
could judge a woman better in her morning gown
than in her evening finery: "We are all good when
we are pleased; but she is the good woman, who
wants not a fiddle to sweeten her." [57] In his
youth he not only danced, but loved—loved a
charming cousin, Theodora Cowper, who loved him
and would have married him; but his utter lack of
worldly prospects and his madness forbade it. In
much later years the gay and gracious Lady Austen, who had lived in close familiarity with him and
Mrs. Unwin, found it convenient to fall in love with
him and nearly caused an unseemly commotion in
that tranquil house. Cowper was obliged to per-
form the delicate task of warning the lady off, which
he did by writing her "a very tender yet resolute
letter, in which he explained and lamented the circumstances that forced him to renounce her society." [58] She burned the letter and troubled him
no more.

But the central attachment of Cowper's life was
that which bound him to Mrs. Unwin. He became
acquainted with the Unwins when he was some-

thing over thirty. Both the husband and the wife attracted him and he soon took up his abode with them, establishing and maintaining the most affectionate relations with the son as well as with the parents. The elder Unwin was killed by a fall from his horse shortly after Cowper became intimate with him. But the poet continued to live with Mrs. Unwin and to profit by her care through all his lingering years of misery. She seems to have been a simply and gently attractive person with no pretension to wit or brilliancy, but shrewdly intelligent, not only in practical matters but in her understanding of Cowper's character and even of his literary work. Cowper's judgment on this point is clear and decisive: "She is a critic by nature, and not by rule, and has a perception of what is good or bad in composition that I never knew deceive her; in so much, that when two sorts of expression have pleaded equally for the preference, in my own esteem, and I have referred, as in such cases I always did, the decision of the point to her, I never knew her at a loss for a just one." [59]

At any rate, it would be hard to overestimate the place Mrs. Unwin filled in Cowper's life. She was but a few years older than he, and the singularity of the relation might have caused comment, and

probably did cause some, in spite of the recognized
dignity and beauty of character in both. At one
time they seriously considered marriage; but the
project was interrupted by one of Cowper's periods
of derangement, and it was never taken up again.
We have no letters addressed to Mrs. Unwin herself since the two were never separated. But the
references in letters to others show the depth of
Cowper's feeling and this is confirmed by the two
poems, the well-known, exquisite sonnet and the
lovely lines asserting the permanence of affection
in age.

> "And still to love, though pressed with ill,
> In wintry age to feel no chill,
> With me is to be lovely still,
> My Mary!"

Mrs. Unwin's death, a few years before the poet's,
greatly augmented the misery of his last days, and
the tender care lavished upon him by others could
never take the place of hers.

As for her feeling for him, there is no written or
spoken word of her own to indicate it to us. But
a bit of his delicate analysis, written to another
friend, shows how fine was the nature of it. "You
are very kind to humor me as you do, and had need
be a little touched yourself with all my oddities,

that you may know how to administer to mine. All whom I love do so, and I believe it to be impossible to love heartily those who do not. People must not do me good *their* way, but in my *own*, and then they do me good indeed." [60] Is it possible to suggest more subtly all that the devotion of such a woman means to such a temperament as Cowper's? Perhaps only a nervous invalid who has had such devotion about him can fully understand it: the perpetual, gentle, unobtrusive watchfulness, the infinite patience with complaint and wearisome and restless questioning, the cheerful disregard of particular symptoms with the boundless sympathy for fundamental causes, the tender rallying, when rallying is best, and the ever-ready consolation when consolation, perhaps unuttered, is most needed—all these Cowper required from his faithful companion, all these he received in unstinted measure.

But the strain for her can also be understood only by those who have endured—or inflicted—something similar. Day and night she was tortured by the endeavor to supply what could not be given, to breathe hope into the hopeless, to furnish comfort where all comfort was impossible. And the climax came when she entered a room and found that her beloved had tried to hang himself and was saved only by her cutting him down. What is humanity made of that it can support such pangs as these and survive?

Yet the woman—and the man—lived on. And we chiefly think of him as we see him in the well-known portrait with the strange turban crowning the sensitive, austere, far-gazing face. He lived and lived, somehow, in that cozy, drowsy atmosphere of English fireside routine. Women petted him, cats purred about him, he held endless skeins of worsted, cracked his little pleasant jokes, drank oceans of tea. And all the time within an inch of his unsteady foot opened that black, unfathomable gulf of hell.

Yet is it not much the same with all of us, with you and me and the man in the street? We laugh and dance and chatter and lie through our trivial daily life, and right beside us yawns the infinite abyss, for all we know with hell at the bottom of it.

VI
CHARLES LAMB

CHRONOLOGY

Charles Lamb
Born, London, February 10, 1775
Educated at Christ's Hospital, 1782-1789
Entered East India House, 1792
Mother killed by Mary, 1796
Pensioned from India House, 1825
Died, Edmonton, December 27, 1834

CHARLES LAMB

I

HE was a creature of whim and frolic fancy, turned life upside down and inside out, sported with it, trifled with it, tossed it in the air like soap bubbles or thistledown, regardless of where it fell or whom it might light upon. He was full of gay jests and mockery, would not take serious things seriously, absolutely refused to, could not: "I was at Hazlitt's marriage, and had like to have been turned out several times during the ceremony. Anything awful makes me laugh. I misbehaved once at a funeral. Yet I can read about these ceremonies with pious and proper feelings. The realities of life only seem the mockeries." [1] Yet in all the mocking there was not one touch of bitterness, nothing whatever of the harsh, acrid wit of Voltaire. There was mischief, infinite mischief, but it was never cruel; and the laughter was always tempered with a possible tear of pity and tenderness.

In other words, no actual figure in literature or history comes nearer to embodying that most exquisite type of Shakespeare's imaginative creation —the court fool or clown, the Touchstones, the Festes, the Fools of Lear. No doubt Shakespeare owed the conception of this dream creature to the crude Vice of the old Moralities. But he turned the original pasteboard puppet into one of the richest and deepest imaginative figures of the world. If you want to realize what he did with it, look at the clowns of his contemporaries, Heywood, Fletcher, Middleton. These are sometimes not unamusing along the old lines; but they are poor, shallow, trivial things after all. Shakespeare took the conventional court fool and made him the incarnation of a novel spiritual attitude. His clowns are not imbecile, not half-witted, the idle occasion of merriment which they only half understand. Their folly is not lack of intelligence but lack of practical selfishness. They understand the so-called wisdom of the world, its long and painful effort—for nothing—its strange propensity to take paste for solid jewels and grave pretence for firm, substantial worth. They know perfectly well what ambition aims at; but they call trifles what mad ambition makes realities, and what the wise esteem trifles

172

are to them as serious as life and death. All things are alike to them, gay, tender, above all questionable. They go about questioning, and smiling because they cannot find the answer. And is not this precisely Charles Lamb? As the fool in a modern play says to the Duke his master:

"I'll tell you this, my lord.
We fools, at least in motley, have wit enough
To manage all men's matters but our own.
We can contrive long plans, lay cunning plots,
Emit sage saws with solemn utterance.
But then there comes some sudden freak, some whim,
And all at once we turn life upside down,
And revel in the wreck with frolic laughter."

On which the Duke queries:

"Can folly know itself?"

And the fool answers:

"It can and does,
And some by that distinguish it from wisdom."

To make Lamb's spiritual attitude more perfect still, and perhaps in part to account for it, we find him set in a background of Elizabethan tragedy such as Shakespeare himself might have chosen for one of his children of folly to interfuse with laughter and tears and wild lyric ecstasy. Up to the time

173

he was twenty Lamb's youth was passed in a setting
of London middle-class life, no doubt prosaic
enough, except as his elfish fancy may have transfigured it from childhood. But in 1796 his sister
Mary, in a fit of frenzy, stabbed his mother to the
heart and Charles could only interfere in time to
snatch the knife away after the deed was done.
What soul could ever escape from such horror as
this, any more than Oedipus could escape from his?
Lamb never did escape it. For forty years he
trod, in a sense, a separate path, earning a meagre
living by office labor, writing delicate bits of prose
and verse as the fancy seized him, above all de-
voting his heart and soul to affectionate attendance
upon the stricken sister who, in her normal days
and months, was an appreciative and sympathetic
companion and most helpful counsellor, but was
torn from him at irregular intervals by returns of
the original malady which made her irresponsible
and dangerous.

It is the haunting, brooding curse of madness, the
family taint of it somewhat affecting Lamb himself, which perhaps more than anything gives him
the strange, wild flavor of the old Shakespearean
type. Even madness could be played with,
could lose something of its terror when you saw it
as, after all, a petty phase of the vast freakishness

CHARLES LAMB

which infected and upheaved the whole universe.
"My life has been somewhat diversified of late. The
six weeks that finished last year and began this,
your very humble servant spent very agreeably in
a madhouse, at Hoxton. I am got somewhat rational now, and don't bite any one. But mad I
was; and many a vagary my imagination played
with me, enough to make a volume, if all were
told." [2] Again, "At some future time I will
amuse you with an account . . . of the strange
turn my frenzy took. I look back upon it at times
with a gloomy kind of envy; for, while it lasted,
I had many, many hours of pure happiness.
Dream not, Coleridge, of having tasted all the
grandeur and wildness of fancy till you have gone
mad." [3]

With this unearthliness, this remoteness even in
the closest contact, this spirit of mocking and mischief, always, always blended with tenderness as
the key-note, we can understand, at least we can
enjoy Lamb's attitude toward the different phases
and interests of human life. Everywhere through
it all I seem to hear Touchstone or Feste singing,

"When that I was and a little tiny boy,
    With hey-ho, the wind and the rain,
A foolish thing was but a toy;
    For the rain, it raineth every day."

175

As for what are commonly reckoned the great matters of the world, it is not to be supposed that such a spirit would take them very seriously. Politics? Of what account are politics in Arden? "Public affairs—except as they touch upon me, and so turn into private,—I cannot whip up my mind to feel any interest in." [4] Titles and dignities, the greatness of the great? How slightly it differs from the littleness of the little! And he disposes of them, whiffs them off like idle feathers with this dainty bit of fooling: "I have published a little book for children on titles of honor; and to give them some idea of the difference of rank and gradual rising, I have made a little scale, supposing myself to receive the following various accessions of dignity . . . —As at first, 1, Mr. C. Lamb; 2, C. Lamb, Esq.; 3, Sir C. Lamb, Bart.; 4, Baron Lamb, of Stamford; 5, Viscount Lamb; 6, Earl Lamb; 7, Marquis Lamb; 8, Duke Lamb. It would look like quibbling to carry it on further, and especially as it is not necessary for children to go beyond the ordinary titles of sub-regal dignity in our own country; otherwise I have sometimes in my dreams imagined myself still advancing, as 9th, King Lamb; 10th, Emperor Lamb; 11th, Pope Innocent; higher than which is nothing upon

earth." [5] Pure nonsense, if you like, childishness, yet such fascinating childishness, and above
all distilling the quintessence of this subtle, original,
mad, lovable, human soul.

Nor do the great thoughts get much more consideration than the great people. It must not be
for a moment supposed that Lamb was really ir-
reverent or scoffing. What is there that counts in
reverence but humility and love? And Lamb was
essentially humble, appreciated his own ignorance
when confronted with the ultimate questions, knew
that he could not answer them though he suspected
that others could answer them little better. As
for love, none ever had more of it than he. But
the ponderous airs of grave philosophers teased him,
the self-sufficiency of surpliced emptiness tormented him. If questions could not be answered,
why ask them? Put them aside, shuffle them off,
drown them with quaint, pretty songs which lull
the tired heart to sleep. The first shock of his
tragic disaster for a moment lashed Lamb into a
serious attitude. Religion was all that counted,
he said, religion would be first to him forever after.
Perhaps there were intensely serious hours in later
years when the madness and the misery recurred.
But in the main dull reflection had to be fooled by

whim or fancy. "Nothing puzzles me more than time and space. Yet nothing puzzles me less, for I never think about them."[6] Creeds, formulas, dogmas? Let others meddle with them, not he. "Friend is married; he has married a Roman Catholic, which has offended his family, but they have come to an agreement, that the boys (if they have children) shall be bred up in the father's religion, and the girls in the mother's, which I think equitable enough. . . . I am determined my children shall be brought up in their father's religion, if they can find out what it is."[7]

II

In the ordinary personal concerns of life, much the same attitude appears as in the larger abstract interests. Perhaps the most serious thing in the world to Lamb was books. "I dream away my life in others' speculations. I love to lose myself in other men's minds. When I am not walking, I am reading; I cannot sit and think. Books think for me."[8] Yet you notice even here it was a question of dreaming. Hard, exact scholarship or study would have been impossible, at any rate it would have meant nothing. Pin him down to a task with books and he would have hated it as he hated any other regularly imposed duty. Books were exquisite when you could trifle and dally with them as a lover with the mistress of a day. Conjugal relations would have been a bore and a burden.

Yet he did love books like a lover, petted them, caressed them, cherished them, collected them with passion and lent them with parsimony, though otherwise most eager to impart his spiritual joys. A book was nothing unless you made a friend of it, took it into your heart, into your life. His Shakespeare, his Beaumont and Fletcher, his Sir Thomas Browne, well thumbed and freely handled —freely but not roughly—who was there in human acquaintance who came quite so near to him as these? "A book reads the better, which is our own, and has been so long known to us, that we know the topography of its blots and dog's ears, and can trace the dirt in it to having read it at tea with buttered muffins, or over a pipe, which I think is the maximum." [9]

As for new books—books of the hour—he read them too, though perhaps with less zeal. Sometimes he treats contemporaries with roughness. Bye, an office mate, has written verses: "They are

chiefly amatory, others of them stupid, the greater
part very far below mediocrity; but they discover
much tender feeling; they are most like Petrarch
of any foreign poet, or what we might have supposed Petrarch would have written, if Petrarch
had been born a fool!" [10] To many of the great
writers of the day he was indifferent. Byron,
Shelley, Moore, Scott did not touch him. His literary dealings with his own friends, Wordsworth,
Coleridge, Southey are nearly perfect. He dis-
cusses everything with the utmost freedom, points
out flaws and weaknesses, or what appear such to
him, with a candor so gentle that it ought never
to have offended, though what author can be
touched without offence? Above all he sympathizes,
enters into his friends' efforts and aspirations as
if they were his own, gives enthusiasm and admiration as heartily to what is well done as if he had
done it himself.

Yet he too was an author, wrote verses of delicate
fancy though far from what one feels that such a
spirit ought somehow to have produced; wrote essays known to every one who knows English literature at all. But even the essays have not quite the
inconsequent, inimitable charm that touches and
colors the letters. So, at least thought Edward

Fitzgerald: "I must say I think his letters infinitely better than his essays," [11] and many will
agree with him. Did Lamb have any consciousness
that some day posterity would read his correspondence with delight? It seems as if he must
have; yet could he have written with more frolic,
ease and naturalness if he had not?

At any rate, as an author he was what he was as
a thinker and liver, a creature of mood and fancy,
impulsive in his ardor and in his repugnance alike.
Not for him the long, careful arrangement of scene
and sequence. "I am the worst hand in the world
at a plot." [12] He toiled at these things, or tried
to toil at them; then they slipped away from his
best endeavor, scattered in glittering fragments,
and he sighed a little and as usual mocked and
smiled: "The damned plot—I believe I must omit
it altogether. The scenes come after one another
like geese, not marshalling like cranes or a Hyde
Park review. The story is as simple as George
Dyer and the language plain as his spouse. The
characters are three women to one man; which is
one more than laid hold on him in the 'Evangely.'
I think that prophecy squinted towards my
drama." [13] Not for him set hours and appointed
tasks, regular engagements at a desk with so much

to be done and delivered according to a systematic schedule. If the whim seized him he would pour out fun and frolic, jests, tears, and merry inversions of the staid commerce of the world in dazzling profusion. But demand these things of him and you struck him as dead as a great reckoning in a little room. "You . . . cannot conceive of the desultory and uncertain way in which I (an author by fits) sometimes cannot put the thoughts of a common letter into sane prose." [14] And when he contracted to do a copy of verses for payment: "I have fretted over them in perfect inability to do them, and have made my sister wretched with my wretchedness for a week together." [15]

As for literary glory, the applause of contemporaries and posterity, well, there certainly never was a more fruitful subject for mocking than this. Authors have their vanity, and you are an author and have it, and must admit it. But that too is easy to make fun of: "A little thing without name will also be printed on the Religion of the Actors, but it is out of your way, so I recommend you, with true author's hypocrisy, to skip it." [16] Then there are the literary women, so reverent, so caressing. The devil of it is that you see them caressing people whom you do not care to be classed with. One of them is inflicted upon Lamb, and he protests: Her "portentous name is *Plura,* in English, 'many things.' Now, of all God's creatures, I detest letters-affecting, authors-hunting ladies. But Fanny 'will have it so.' So Miss Many-Things and I are to have a conference, of which you shall have the result." [17] And all the time the pretty girls, the gay girls, the kind of girls you adore, are quite indifferent to your prestige and your glory. You see them pass you, and you sigh at the irrelevance of things: "To me she was a vision of Genteel Comedy realized. Those kind of people never come to see one." [18]

But if Lamb was more or less indifferent to the sweets of literary fame, its bitters afflicted him as they do all of us. He worshiped the theatre. He would have liked above everything to write plays. But somehow those wretched plots eluded him and laughed at him. His tragedy is no more than readable, if readable. His comedy, from which he hoped so much, fell flat. The audience hissed him roundly. But he got even with them before posterity by the wildest, maddest page on hissing that ever crept into comedy or tragedy either. That God should have given his creatures mouths to kiss with and "that they should turn them into mouths of adders, bears, wolves, hyenas, and whistle like tempests, and emit breath through them like distillations of aspic poison, to asperse and vilify the innocent labors of their fellow-creatures who are desirous to please them!" [19]

Evidently, if money was required for the necessities of life, Lamb was not the man to get it by playwriting or to any extent by authorship of any kind. In matters of money it is notable that for all his laughter and all his general carelessness he was exactly conscientious. His means were most limited and he had to exercise rigid thrift and was always on the lookout for ways of increasing them. How perfectly human is this sigh of his, how appropriate to all of us, rich and poor alike: "In fact, if I got or could but get £50 a year only, in addition to what I have, I should live in affluence." [20] Yet he trifled with money difficulties and limitations as with other things, and in trifling he emitted many an exquisite paradox of wisdom, as Touchstone might have. "My motto is, 'contented with little, yet wishing for more.'" [21] Could life have a better one?

As for generosity, it is hardly necessary to say that he abounded in it. Formal, theoretical philanthropy seemed to him to lend itself occasionally to

184

satire. Who will deny that he was right or fail to
see the point of his decision to inquire of a local
stonecutter the price of a simple monument on
which should be inscribed "Here C. Lamb loved
his brethren of mankind"? "Everybody will come
there to love," he says.[22] But when it came to
putting his hand unobtrusively into his pocket to
help a fellow author, to making one of those loans,
conveniently so-called, which enable the shiftless to
live at the expense of the frugal, he never failed,
though even here he must have his jest: "Heaven
does not owe me sixpence for all I have given, or
lent (as they call it), to such importunity; I only
gave it because I could not bear to refuse it; and I
have done good by my weakness." [23]

For the generosity, as well as for the daily needs,
money had to be found somehow and Lamb found
it mainly by drudgery in the office of the East
India Company, where he toiled for many years.
He hated it, of course. There are probably few
men who like daily clerkship at a desk, routine
labor of which the benefit appears mainly to inure
to others. Still some spirits, born to regularity,
take to the habit and hardly long for anything else.
But a quivering, wavering, flitting, tumultuous
soul like Lamb's could not have been more hope-

lessly out of place. No doubt he did the work and did it well. But he took his revenge in quipping and quibbling about it, mocking the work and the workers and all the endless conventional process of the world's support. Accounts? How he hated accounts, long, stupid rows of figures to be added and added to the end of time! Drudgery? Hours of drudgery? Days of drudgery? Oh, to escape it, to forget it, to fling it into the bottomless pit of oblivion! "Darling laziness! heaven of Epicurus! Saint's Everlasting Rest! That I could drink vast potations of thee through unmeasured Eternity— *Otium cum, vel sine dignitate.*" [24] Then the emptiness of it all, the formal pretence! These solemn creatures painfully gathering themselves together day after day to pretend to do in eight hours what might just as well be done in one! The very mention of a holiday is horrible to them: a holiday would only show how unnecessary it all is. "The Committee have formally abolished all holydays whatsoever—for which may the Devil, who keeps no holydays, have them in his eternal burning workshop." [25] The routine, the endless, deadly monotony do get on a gay clown's spirits so that the sweet of life is almost crushed out of him: "My theory is to enjoy life, but my practice is against it.

I grow ominously tired of official confinement." [26]
Yet he dares not rebel, he dares not resist. That
fatal bread and butter must come from some-
where, and from where if not from the India Office?
So he submits and obeys, but always with that de-
licious whimsical sigh of protest: "I come, I come.
Don't drag me so hard by the hair of my head,
Genius of British India. I know my hour is come,
Faustus must give up his soul, O Lucifer, O
Mephistopheles!" [27]

Then the strange yet so perfectly human reversal
appears. He escapes from his bonds, gets at last
his little pension to ensure him against absolute
want, leaves the office behind and goes free. And
behold—freedom is not all he thought it would be.
To be sure there is at first an elastic rebound. His
days, his hours are all his own, there are vast oceans
of leisure revealing themselves before him over
which he can navigate his light ship with every
dancing wind that blows. There is unmeasured
reading, and unmeasured writing, and long walks
in the country, and gay and social converse just
when and as you please. Yet somehow when you
can have it all at will the savor is gone out of it.
The hours, which seemed so painfully full are now
as painfully empty. You look in at the office to

laugh at them drudging wearily, and all at once you are amazed to find that you wish you were back. For years you have sung the praises of idleness. Now you are almost tempted into hymns that deify the virtues of work. "I pity you for over-work; but I assure you no work is worse. The mind preys on itself, the most unwholesome food. I bragged formerly that I could not have too much time. I have a surfeit. . . . I am a sanguinary murderer of time, and would kill him inch-meal just now. But the snake is vital." [28] So humanity trembles backward and forward, always longing for something different and never satisfied.

It might be thought that at least the change from office to out-of-doors would be beneficial to health. Perhaps it was. Yet the change from habits to no habits for a man of Lamb's temperament may have been injurious. The letters have a good deal about health in them, as is natural for all of us in writing to friends. It does not appear that Lamb was especially an invalid. But he was sensitive, high-strung, a bundle of nerves. Like so much in the "Essays," the study of "Night-Fears" is no doubt highly autobiographical; "I was dreadfully alive to nervous terrors. The night-time, solitude, and the dark, were my hell. The sufferings I endured in this nature would justify the expression." Persons so constituted are not likely to know abounding, self-forgetful health at any time. Strange, unaccountable depressions and miseries overcome them like summer clouds, and to such Lamb was evidently too often liable. But with ill health as with other things, the true secret was to laugh it away. Lamb mocked at his own miseries with unhesitating, unmerciful wit, and he gently trifled with those of others with the light and wayward glee of his frolicsome revelry. What a wild piece of mirth is the long letter in which he cheers up Robinson's sufferings by pretending that they are his own.[29]

III

In all his mockery and in all his seriousness, in his business and in his leisure, it is clear that what first and always interested Charles Lamb was the human heart. *"Up* to anything; *down* to everything; whatever *sapit hominem*. A perfect man,"[30] is his description of a dear friend: it fits himself. New lives, new thoughts, new habits, new manners stimulated and excited him. The very suggestion of foreign travel, which was so remote from his stay-at-home ways, elicits an outcry of un-the longing for it: "I have often wished I had lived in the golden age, when shepherds lay stretched upon flowers, and roused themselves at their leisure, —the genius there is in a man's natural idle face, that has not learned his multiplication table!" [36] But green fields were monotonous, and mountains looked down upon you, and birds sang the same thing over. If you planned an excursion and counted upon a pleasant time, you got a wetting. Wordsworth might sing the country if he chose: it was his stock in trade. But persons of a different habit of thought could not always join him. And to Wordsworth, of all men, Lamb frankly wrote his opinions on the subject: "My attachments are all local, purely local. I have no passion (or have had none since I was in love, and then it was the spurious engendering of poetry and books) for groves and valleys. . . . Your sun, and moon, and skies, and hills and lakes, affect me no more, or scarcely come to me in more venerable characters, than as a gilded room with tapestry and tapers, where I might live with handsome visible objects. I consider the clouds above me but as a roof beautifully painted, but unable to satisfy the mind." [37]

Yes, he was a child of the city, of great, enthralling, inexhaustible London: he knew it and recog-

nized it. The hubbub and tumult delighted him,
kept him stimulated and excited, took him out of
himself. The noise and hurry and dirt which
wearied and disgusted spirits like Gray and Fitzgerald were to Lamb a constant intoxication.
When his foot was on his native pavement he was
himself, and then only. "The wonder of these
sights impels me into night-walks about her
crowded streets, and I often shed tears in the motley Strand from fullness of joy at so much life." [38]
To sit at a window and watch the ever-shift-
ing current of little accidents and incidents was
endlessly diverting. Trifles are the delight of the
true clown spirit because they are not really trifles
at all, but go down to the depths of the world if
you reflect upon them idly. Was ever the note of
city variety and immensity better caught than in
this tumultuous passage? "The lighted shops of
the Strand and Fleet Street; the innumerable
trades, tradesmen, and customers, coaches, wag-
ons, playhouses; all the bustle and wickedness
round about Covent Garden; the very women of
the town; the watchmen, drunken scenes, rattles;
life awake, if you awake, at all hours of the night;
the impossibility of being dull in Fleet Street; the
crowds, the very dirt and mud, the sun shining

off in scenes like the inimitable visit of Miss Ben-jay,[44] which for comic richness cannot be surpassed by Sterne or Fielding.

Yet Lamb enjoyed the people he liked, wanted them, longed for them. The strange mixture of social feelings is admirably caught in his complaint of visitors who neither come nor go to suit his wishes. "Come, never, I would say to these spoilers of my dinner; but if you come, never go." [45] When those he longed for came, he made them feel at home, made himself delightful, overflowed with the wit and chat and the endless effervescence of drollery which make the charm of the letters. While enjoying himself thoroughly he imparted enjoyment to others, and there is no finer secret of social success.

In liking to have his friends about him he liked the social adjuncts of such society. He liked good eating and played with it and reveled with it men-tally even more than physically. Gifts are sent him, of game, of fruit, of tidbits of all sorts. What rollicking, roystering letters he writes in return! A good dinner and a good friend to share it with, what can life give more? His eccentricities in the matter of pig are among the treasures of literature, and the "Roast Pig" essay is far better known than

196

some that are deeper and sweeter. But the riot of mirthful words on porcine delicacies in the letters is more fascinating even than the essay. "Not that *I* sent the pig, or can form the remotest guess what part Owen could play in the business. I never knew him give anything away in my life. . . . To confess an honest truth, a pig is one of those things which I could never think of sending away. . . . Where the fine feeling of benevolence giveth a higher smack than the sensual rarity, there my friends (or any good man) may command me; but pigs are pigs, and I myself therein am nearest to myself." [46]

Drink was the natural accompaniment of eating, even had its charm when eating could be dispensed with. And drink was the natural enemy, the dearest foe of Lamb. His light, fine, unstable, fantastic brain was too easily overset. Draughts that would have merely stimulated others muddled him, and, consequently, among the sadly disposed who did not understand, he got the credit of disreputable intemperance, a notion not diminished by "The Confessions of a Drunkard," which has just enough of the autobiographical to mislead. There was a constant battle, a constant resistance, a constant yielding, which continued to the end and which furnished the strangest matter for the jesting spirit that jested at all things. Among the very last of Lamb's letters is the singular outburst to Cary apologizing for the lamentable and regretted excesses of a previous evening, yet apologizing as only a genius or an angel could apologize.

So with tobacco. Both the stimulus and the repose of it were appealing, enchanting to Lamb's nerves. "A pipe and a comedy of Fletcher's the last thing of a night is the best recipe for light dreams, and to scatter away nightmares." [47] An old pipe was comfort, and hope, and peace; at times it seemed that you could suck a bit of heaven through it. Yet it must be admitted that "there is no tipple nor tobacco in the grave whereunto he hasteneth." [48] Even on earth it meant indigestion and nerves and endless trouble. It was better to put it away. So he put it away, he was always putting it away, bidding farewell to it in verse and in sadness; finally he did put it away.[49] But, oh, the struggle! He could not have carried it through if he had not laughed at it.

Again, take the ethereal side of human relations in contrast to the purely physical. The love of woman may be the most—or least—ethereal of all. What did Lamb know about it? Enough, it appears obscurely, when he was young. There are bits of reminiscence through the letters, trifles of mirth and mocking, like Touchstone's tender recollection of Jane Smile, "the kissing of her batlet and the cow's dugs that her pretty chopt hands had milked." There are hints of more serious passion, as of the young Quaker whom he was in love with "for some years while I lived at Pentonville, though I had never spoken to her in my life," [50] or in regard to the burning of the "little journal of my foolish passion which I had a long time kept." [51] Also at a later period Lamb wished to marry Miss Kelly, the actress, who rejected him. But in the main madness and misery and Mary and the ill-paidi drudgery of the India Office made marriage seem impracticable.

But the love of friends was far more satisfying than the furious, frail adoration of Venus, and in the former Lamb indulged to the fullest and richest extent. Rarely has friendship cast a larger, sweeter glamor over a collection of letters than it does over his. There is, as always, the mocking; but such delicious, tender, quaint, graceful mocking: never a flaw of bitterness or harshness in it. Even his distinguished literary friends, for whose intelligence and genius he has the profoundest admira-

tion, do not escape. There is the exquisite definition of Coleridge, "an archangel, a little damaged." [52] And the solemn Wordsworth is twitched
and twisted, just as if he were a playmate at school.
"He says he does not see much difficulty in writing
like Shakespeare, if he had a mind to try it. It is
clear that nothing is wanting but the mind." [53]

As for lesser personages, who undeniably lend
themselves to the comic touch, Lamb's gaiety with
them is unlimited. Take the Cottle brothers. "To
the expediency of this measure Cottle fully as-
sented, but could not help adding that he always
thought that the qualities of his brother's heart ex-
ceeded those of his head. I believe his brother,
when living, had formed precisely the same idea of
him; and I apprehend the world will assent to both
judgments." [54] Or there is George Dyer. Lamb
makes of him a comic figure as rich, as original, as enduring, and as lovable as Parson Adams
or Uncle Toby. The whole long letter to Manning, written in August, 1800, is but a delicious
unfolding of the foibles and oddities of this singular creature, yet all done with such gentleness that
you cannot fail to feel the love at the bottom. And
it ends, "God bless his dear absurd head!" [55]

For Lamb loved Cottle, and he loved Dyer, and

he loved all of them. He could mock even at the depth of abstract affection, so much did he hate to pretend, to feign, to strain after the conventional friendships of the world. "Why did you give it me? I do not like you enough to give you anything so good." [56] But his friends knew that he would give them anything, even his vast, fly-away, intangible, illimitable soul if he could have done it. In his youth we find a subtlety of analysis which shows what he had thought and felt: "There is a monotony in the affections, which people living together, or, as we do now, very frequently seeing each other, are apt to give in to; a sort of indifference in the expression of kindness for each other, which demands that we should sometimes call to our aid the trickery of surprise." [57] In his age he speaks of an attachment of childhood with a tenderness that goes almost too deep for tears: "He was my friend and my father's friend all the life I can remember. I seem to have made foolish friendships ever since. Those are friendships which outlive a second generation. . . . To the last he called me Charley. I have none to call me Charley now." [58]

This profound, underlying, unfathomable goodness and nobleness in Lamb must never be forgotten in the enjoyment of his frolicsome mirth, his clownish buffoonery as it seemed to some excellent souls. The two are really always bound up together and the nobleness is ready to surge up at any moment. The common daily duties of life, however disliked, are done without complaining, sometimes with humorous rebellion, but done, and done well. Obligations of toil, obligations of money are respected to the point of scruple. Cash may be short, often owing to the needs of friends, but there is no whining and no remissness. Lamb was no Sheridan, no Micawber to sponge on acquaintances or strangers. Surely a man has a right to smile when his bills are paid.

And then there was always that untiring devotion to the few whom he loved. There might be occasional frank criticism, and the frankness might lead to temporary estrangement. But there was the great enfolding tenderness through it all. Manning, Coleridge, Wordsworth, Barton, not to speak of others, were part of Lamb's heart.

Chief of all was Mary. Of his elder brother John, Charles speaks with brotherly regard; but evidently no such relation obtained as between the younger brother and sister. The story of Lamb's intimate companionship with Mary, of his unfaltering loyalty to her in every aspect of illness or health is essential to the understanding of his character. The Fool in Lear did not love more; and is not his love ideal in its self-forgetfulness? And Mary deserved the love and gave as much as she got. Nobody could have understood better than she those strange, fascinating, afflicting nerves, which quivered daily with the passion and the laughter and the infinite questioning of the universe. Just because she was so soothing and so sympathetic when she was normal, the black shadow which tore them absolutely apart was all the more horrible when it came. Lamb watched over her, provided for her, did all that love could do to make life tolerable. Yet at times he could but long for relief, for her sake: "My head is quite bad. I almost wish that Mary were dead. God bless you!" [59] And then he reproached himself for indifference, for irritability: "I know I have been wasting and teasing her life for five years past incessantly with my cursed drinking and ways of going on." [60] Yet the very reproach was, as so often, the best evidence of the devotion, and many other words show what her companionship meant and what it meant to be deprived of her: "All my strength is gone, and I am like a fool, bereft of her co-operation. I dare not think, lest I should think wrong; so used am I to look up to her in the least and the biggest perplexity. . . . She is older and wiser and better than I, and all my wretched imperfections I cover to myself by resolutely thinking on her goodness. She would share life and death, heaven and hell, with me." [61]   And what could love ask or give more?

Edward Fitzgerald, who appreciated Lamb as much as any one, records a remark of Thackeray's: " 'Saint Charles,' as Thackeray once called him, while looking at one of his half-mad letters, and remembering his devotion to that quite mad sister." [62] And again, " 'Saint Charles,' said Thackeray to me thirty years ago, putting one of C. L.'s letters to his forehead." [63]   And Lamb may well be a saint to those who feel that the insoluble mystery of the universe is in no way better solved than by the two delicately related keys of love and laughter.

VII
JOHN KEATS

CHRONOLOGY

John Keats

Born, London, October 29, 1795

Apprenticed to a surgeon at Edmonton, 1810

Endymion published, 1818

Isabella, etc., published, 1820

Sailed for Italy, autumn of 1820

Died, Rome, February 23, 1821

JOHN KEATS

I

THOUGH Keats burned his life out at twenty-five, consumed by the passion for creating great poetry, he was no visionary, no cracked-brained dreamer, but a sane, sound, normal human being, as Shakespeare was. Until tuberculosis extinguished him in his Roman exile under the care of the devoted Severn in 1821, he had knocked round the London and the England of the early nineteenth century, had met men and women, had studied medicine, though his natural sensibility made it difficult for him to practice it, had seen life and faced it and enjoyed it. He had indeed the Shakespearean zest for life, quite independent of literature, and was human enough himself to enter into all the humanity of others. And he was ready to endure life as well as to enjoy it: "The first thing that strikes me on hearing a misfortune having befallen another is this—'Well, it cannot be helped:

he will have the pleasure of trying the resources of his spirit.' " [1] He had the pleasure—or the discipline—of trying the resources of his spirit enormously, and he knew the significance of the words he put into the mouth of his old Titan:

"Oh, folly! For to bear all naked ills,
And to envisage circumstance all calm,
That is the top of sovereignty." [2]

Much of this broad human dignity, this calm self-possession may surely be read in Keats's face. Even in youth the grave brow and the penetrating eyes have infinite nobleness.

Let us follow this daily, sunlit humanity of Keats in some of the more ordinary phases and common interests of life. Before his illness overcame him it is clear that he had a good share in all natural, simple sports and activities. He liked to ramble in the country, to take long walks and walking journeys, with an eye out always for the amusing vagaries of men and women. He liked boating: "For the last five or six days, we have had regularly a boat on the Isis, and explored all the streams about, which are more in number than your eyelashes." [3] He even looked out for wider exploration, and planned to visit his brother in

America. He could play cards or dance with real pleasure, as shows in his comment on another: "Rice said he cared less about the hour than any one, and the proof is his dancing—he cares not for time, dancing as if he was deaf." [4] Also he could fight, when necessary, as appears from his thrashing a butcher's boy who was acting the bully.

Nor was this high-strung, sensitive poet by any means above the more sensuous pleasures of humanity. He liked good eating and said so with the utmost frankness. Partridge appealed to him as it does to the more prosaic: "I forgot game—I must plead guilty to the breast of a partridge, the back of a hare, the backbone of a grouse, the wing and side of a pheasant and a woodcock *passim*." [5] And he liked the food washed down with good liquor. Even the grosser forms were not rejected. Whiskey? There is something to be said for whiskey. But claret was his special delight, and he refers to it repeatedly: "For really 'tis so fine—it fills one's mouth with a gushing freshness—then goes down cool and feverless—then you do not feel it quarreling with your liver—no, it is rather a peacemaker, and lies as quiet as it did in the grape." [6] He even lets it at times get the better of him, rather deliberately: "We had a claret feast some little while ago. . . . We all got a little tipsy —but pleasantly so—I enjoy claret to a degree." [7] Which does not mean that he was in any possible sense a winebibber.

Before tuberculosis struck him, he seems to have had health sufficient to meet all reasonable demands upon it. No doubt his demands were not always reasonable and the carelessness of youth hastened and accentuated the end. The importance of health, what it meant, how absolutely necessary it was for achieving the great things he aimed at, he understood as well as any one. "Nothing is so bad as want of health—it makes one envy scavengers and cinder-sifters," he cried when he had lost it. [8] But he did not need to lose it to appreciate it. He advises others most judiciously as to the care of it, and he sighs over the sense of what its fulness and perfection would do for him: "I think if I had a free and healthy and lasting organization of heart, and lungs as strong as an ox's so as to be able to bear unhurt the shock of extreme thought and sensation without weariness, I could pass my life very nearly alone though it should last eighty years." [9]

In the most practical and necessary of all life's concerns, if not the most interesting or inviting, money and business, Keats does not appear to have

been wholly shrewd or successful. With his tastes
and tendencies there was a constant temptation to
spend, and as he was situated there was little for
spending. He expresses an indifference and disregard to money which are noble and admirable:
"It may be a proud sentence; but by Heaven I am
as entirely above all matters of interest as the sun
is above the earth." [10] Unfortunately one cannot
live wholly without it, however. There were bills
to be paid which were most pressing and most annoying. Also there was the constant importunity
and the constant need of friends, and it is notable
how greatly Keats was involved in supplying these,
how the impecunious seemed to turn to him, and
how much of his financial distress was connected
with the effort to take care of them. "When I
offered you assistance I thought I had it in my
hand; I thought I had nothing to do but to do. . . .
I assure you I have harassed myself ten times more
than if I alone had been concerned in so much gain
or loss." [11] To which it should be added that
his friends were equally ready to help him and to
stand by him in his needs and difficulties. But it
should further be appreciated that whether he
spent or whether he lent or whether he borrowed,
he was scrupulous and conscientious, knew his obli-

gations and tried to fulfil them, and wished others
to understand that it was so. He writes to his publishers: "I am sure you are confident of my re-
sponsibility, and in the sense of squareness that is
always in me." [12] We could not ask a poet, or
a man of business, to be more practical than that.

These financial relations show how intimately
Keats's life was bound up with that of others, and
it is impossible not to feel that in his general human
dealings he was as fundamentally sane and normal
as in other respects. To be sure, he was always
busy, intensely preoccupied with great hopes that
life was not long enough to realize, and the little
distractions that humanity carries with it were
sometimes vexatious. A houseful of children may
be charming, but it is not conducive to work: "The
servant has come for the little Browns this morning—they have been a toothache to me which I shall
enjoy the riddance of— Their little voices are
like wasps' stings— Sometimes am I all wound
with Browns." [13] Moreover, like most self-conscious persons he was shy and diffident, immensely
aware of his own self in any social gathering and inclined to exaggerate the importance of
that self to others, who probably thought little
about it. "Think of my pleasure in solitude in

JOHN KEATS

comparison of my commerce with the world—there
I am a child. . . . Some think me middling, others
silly, others foolish—every one thinks he sees my
weak side against my will, when in truth it is with
my will. . . . This is one great reason why they
like me so; because they can all show to advantage
in a room and eclipse from a certain tact one who
is reckoned to be a good poet." [14] Possibly the
analysis was not correct: it certainly cannot have
been helpful to freedom of intercourse.

Yet this man, whose work was to be built upon
the passions of men, liked to see them, to converse
with them, to get close to them and feel the intimate
warmth of humanity. He likes to watch a busy
crowd and trace the interplay of motives and petty
vanities, as in his vivid description of the life behind the scenes of a theatre.[15] He likes to meet
notable individuals, such as Wordsworth and
Coleridge, and renders the strange medley of the
latter's talk with shrewd appreciation.[16] And he
likes to mingle in a gay company just for the
pure amusement of it, to take jests and to make
them. He likes a mad burst of frolic that sweeps
carelessly into the small hours of the morning, likes
to shake off restraint and go free and forget. He
has a relish for pure nonsense, fills his letters with

a riotous fun which is often youthful and crude and ill-digested, has not reached the delicacy and fineness of Lamb, and when it took actual literary form, as in "The Cap and Bells," was apt to be somewhat heavy and labored. But it must have made him very charming company when he felt thoroughly at home and forgot himself. The elements of a full and rich social life were about him somewhere.

As for closer friendship and affection, the warmth and humanity of his nature perhaps show in these most of all. He not only lent his friends money, he gave them tenderness and thoughtfulness and advice which was always well-meant and intelligent and sometimes useful and profitable. He seems especially to have had an earnest interest in patching up their quarrels. Apparently he was not a quarreler himself, took too large a view of life and human nature. But his friends spatted and fought and abused and accused each other. And again and again he set himself to apply that practical common-sense which he had so abundantly and which is the best cure for quarrels by simply dissipating them. His vision was too clear for him to feel that humanity was always estimable: "Whatever people on the other side of the question may advance, they cannot deny that they are always surprised at hearing of a good action, and never of a bad one." [17]   But he knew well that men might be loved, even if they could not be esteemed.

Above all, his tenderness flowed out to his own family. His father and mother died in his youth, but his brothers and sister and sister-in-law were objects of constant and peculiar regard, and the devotion with which he nursed the brother who died was equal to that afterwards shown by Severn to himself.

II

But what is most striking about this born poet in all these daily matters and relations of life is the richness and splendor of imagination with which he transfused and interpenetrated even the commonest things. All readers of his poetry are familiar with this quality and the poetry would amply suffice to illustrate it. But his letters are at once less known and more personal, and the glow and glamor of imagination touches them everywhere as it does the poems. Often in the middle of a letter he burst right into verse. Or he brings in his memories of Shakespeare and other poets till it is difficult to tell where they end and he begins. He himself marks this element of his correspondence and enlarges upon it delightfully: "If I scribble long letters I must play my vagaries—I must be too heavy, or too light, for whole pages—I must be quaint and free of tropes and figures—I must play my draughts as I please, and for my advantage and your erudition, crown a white with a black, or a black with a white, and move into black or white, far and near as I please." [18] In no other letter writer except Flaubert is this play, this wonderful flash and glory of imagination at once so abundant and spontaneous.

Even in the comparatively prosaic concerns which we have hitherto been dealing with, sport, health, money, eating and drinking, the imagination finds ample chance to spread its glorifying color. Take the most humdrum of all, money, and see how at once imagination sets to work on it, transfiguring currency into a strange figment of fantastic purport and illimitable suggestion: "I am extremely indebted to you for your liberality in the shape of manufactured rag, value £20, and shall immediately proceed to destroy some of the minor heads of that hydra the dun; to conquer which the knight need have no sword, shield, cuirass, cuisses, herbadgeon, spear, casque, greaves, paldrons, spurs, chevron, or any other scaly commodity, but he need only take the bank-note of faith and cash of salvation, and set out against the monster." [19] Even so the Elizabethan fancy played with the dull surface of life and made gold of it. Or take a larger comment on the sordid and troublesome course of daily affairs and their blend and mixture: "Circumstances are like clouds continually gathering and bursting. While we are laughing, the seed of some trouble is put into the wide arable land of events. While we are laughing, it sprouts, it grows, and suddenly bears a poison fruit which we must pluck." [20]

And if imagination can so trifle with familiar matter of today, it is easy to see how wide will be its range in larger concerns that more naturally appeal to it. The plastic arts were not much within the range of Keats's study or competence. Yet here also it is evident that his æsthetic sensibility reacted with singular passionate ardor, and imagination could hardly play more richly than it did about his "Grecian Urn." So with music. His technical knowledge and experience were no doubt small. But the instant a musical suggestion touches him it gets interwoven with a range of thought and feeling far beyond the immediate present: "The simple imaginative mind may have its reward in the repetition of its own silent working coming continually on the spirit with a fine suddenness—to compare great things with small, have you never, by being surprised with an old melody, in a delicious place by a delicious voice, *felt* over again your very speculations and surmises at the time it first operated on your soul?" [21]   And from this imaginative point of view was ever anything better said than

> "Heard melodies are sweet, but those unheard
> Are sweeter?" [22]

When it comes to the realm of external nature, where no technical training is needed but simply eyes and ears and emotions, the exuberance of Keats's imaginative activity is unbounded. Of all the great qualities of his poetry this is perhaps the greatest. It works as much through the chaotic luxuriance of "Endymion" as in the concentrated beauty of his great odes and sonnets. The "Autumn," the "Nightingale," the "Grecian Urn" contain the finest rendering of Nature in the English language. From "fast-fading violets" to "earnest stars" there is no natural object that is not transfigured and transported into the realm of imperishable beauty.

But here too the letters afford a more personal and intimate phase of the same passionate familiarity and rapture. Sometimes it is a broad and almost comic handling of more superficial aspects, say a trip through Devonshire blighted and thwarted by perpetual rain. The weather is played with, tossed about and tumbled, made to yield infinite suggestion of riotous and complex merriment, all the time with a background of light and shade and color and possible ecstasy.[23] Sometimes natural objects are converted with Shakespearean alchemy into their human spiritual equivalents. There is the spider's web, when "she fills the air with a beautiful circuiting. Man should be content with as few points to tip with the fine web of his soul, and weave a tapestry empyrean—full of symbols for his spiritual eye, of softness for his spiritual touch, of space for his wandering, of distinctness for his luxury." [24] Or again there is a flare of splendor when the whole universe is laid under contribution to appease our mortal misery: "In truth, the great elements we know of, are no mean comforters: the open sky sits upon our senses like a sapphire crown—the air is our robe of state—

the earth is our throne, and the sea a mighty min-
strel playing before it—able, like David's harp, to
make such a one as you forget almost the tempest
cares of life." [25]   Finally there is the complete
loss of self in the natural world, the effacement of
this tormented, questioning, haunting, discontented
individuality in the vaster movements or even in the
petty trifles of the life outside. As it is put more
grandly in "Hyperion,"

> "I am but a voice;
> My life is but the life of winds and tides,
> No more than winds and tides can I avail," [26]

or with the lightest, simplest touch in the letters:
"I scarcely remember counting upon any happiness. I look not for it if it be not in the present
hour: nothing startles me beyond the moment.
The setting sun will always set me to rights, or if a
sparrow come before my window, I take part in its
existence and pick about the gravel." [27]

When Keats touches books, reading, especially
poetry, there is the same transfiguration as with
natural objects. The passionate enthusiasm of the
reader colors and glorifies everything that is read;
for, with such a temperament, naturally little is
read that is not susceptible to color and glory. Let

others meddle with science and statistics. Perhaps if we chose we could make our way here too. But with all the splendor of past genius before us why should we choose anything of such a dull and plodding bent? Poetry? What is life without it? "I find I cannot exist without poetry, without eternal poetry; half the day will not do, the whole of it. I began with a little, but habit has made me a Leviathan." [28] And he indulges in wild, rich, wandering speculations as to the eternal nature of beauty. Again he pours out his rapture over favorite authors, as in the Chapman sonnet, or that written before re-reading "King Lear." Shakespeare, Spenser, Burton, or perhaps the new revelation of contemporary writers—life is not long enough to revel in them.

In the more practical prosaic aspects of general human affairs it was hardly to be expected that this ideal temper should take a great interest, especially in its early twenties. Keats lived in more or less intimate literary association with Hunt and his radical group, and the prejudice against them perhaps extended itself to him, even coloring the critical reviews of his work. But nothing could be more unjust. He was radical in the sense that he went to the roots of things. But he was far indeed from any disposition to active interference with the conduct of public matters. In politics, as in everything else, it was the imaginative aspect that touched him, and his idea of democracy is not quite that of the average social reformer: "Man should not dispute or assert, but whisper results to his neighbor, and thus by every germ of spirit sucking the sap from mould ethereal every human being might become great, and humanity instead of being a wide heath of furze and briars, with here and there a remote oak or pine, would become a grand democracy of forest trees." [29]

Toward the larger, deeper spiritual concerns of life and death Keats's attitude is much the same, but more intense. The eager petulance and irreverence of youth affected him as it has others, and he poured it out in the early sonnet:

"The church bells tolled a melancholy round,
Calling the people to some other prayers,
Some other gloominess, more dreadful cares,
More hearkening to the sermon's horrid sound." [30]

Yet this mood was temporary and never touched him deeply. He was no more essentially destructive in speculative thought than he was in politics. More and more his mind played constructively and creatively round the great problems. But what is large and fine about him is his distaste for dogmatic conclusions in speculative matters. Like Flaubert in this as in so many other points, he felt that life and beauty were too rich and vital to be netted, tangled, strangled in theories or systems. Always to be thinking, to be feeling, to be reaching out, grasping for more truth, more splendor—that was the ideal: "The only means of strengthening one's intellect is to make up one's mind about nothing—to let the mind be a thoroughfare for all thoughts, not a select party." [31] Especially, one should not argue for the sake of arguing: "I shall never be a reasoner, because I care not to be in the right, when retired from bickering and in a proper philosophical temper." [32] And with abstract thought as with concrete experience, what counts most and is most original is the glory of the imaginative garment which not only adorns but illuminates and stimulates.

III

When the imagination is so significant, so dominating an element of mental make-up, it is inevitably much concerned with itself, and this was characteristic of Keats from an early period. He dwelt upon the imaginative power, analyzed it, dissected it with extraordinary subtlety and insight, not merely as a distinguishing gift of his own but in its essential nature. The remarkable page of the letter to Woodhouse of October, 1818, should be read entire to appreciate how close and passionate this analysis was: "A poet is the most unpoetical of anything in existence, because he has no identity— he is continually in, for, and filling some other body. The sun, the moon, the sea, and men and women, who are creatures of impulse, are poetical, and have about them an unchangeable attribute; the poet has none, no identity: he is certainly the most unpoetical of all God's creatures." [33]

Again, such an imagination would not be content with merely analyzing itself; it would be restlessly, eternally eager to project itself in some definite achievement of creative beauty. With Keats the eagerness was so constant, so intense that it became interwoven with almost all his waking and sleeping thought. To create beauty, to pour out unlimited splendor that would stir the world and live, this idea took possession of him in childhood and never left him. "I am one that 'gathers samphire, dreadful trade': the cliff of poesy towers above me." [34] "I had become all in a tremble from not having written anything of late: the sonnet overleaf did me good." [35] So he writes, boyishly but with sincerity; and so he wrote till death.

No doubt the element of success, of reputation, of popularity entered in. Like most great writers Keats had his times of disclaiming this. The mere unthinking applause of the mob irritated him, its acceptance of momentary fashions, its utter inability to distinguish the true and permanent from the merely glittering that must shortly fade away. He speaks of "The solitary indifference I feel for applause, even from the finest spirits." [36] With remote pride he rejects the adulation of the crowd even when he feels that he can win it: "I feel it in my power to become a popular writer. I feel it in my power to refuse the poisonous suffrage of a public." [37] Yet after all there is something in leaving "great verse unto a little clan" [38] something in being "rich in the simple worship of a day." [39] And it is with a fine, high, confident security that he declares: "I think I shall be among the English Poets after my death." [40]

At any rate, whether one cared for fame or not, one could labor to deserve it, to do things that men ought to admire if they admired at all. Not that

Keats was one of the writers who proceed mechanically, doing set tasks at stated hours, so many lines and so many pages, whether the spirit responds or not. On the contrary, there were times when the impulse swept down upon him, took possession of him; when great ideas and rich utterance poured through him like a torrent and he had to strive with them or die. There were other hours of large, contented leisure when he asked nothing but to absorb, without even the definite consciousness of doing that. He was splendidly capable of fruitful indolence. "This morning I am in a sort of temper, indolent and supremely careless. . . . My passions are all asleep, from my having slumbered till nearly eleven, and weakened the animal fibre all over me, to a delightful sensation, about three degrees on this side of faintness. If I had teeth of pearl and the breath of lilies I should call it languor, but as I am I must call it laziness." [41]

Nor again did he toil with the endless scrupulous patience of a Flaubert to make every line and every word impossibly perfect. He felt that, with genius of his type at any rate, such minute toil would imperil spontaneity, that the bent and the impulse must be taken as they came with a serene confidence in the compelling deity and an assurance that out of comparative imperfection a higher perfection would in the end appear. How admirable is the well-known letter to Hessey, written after the severe criticism of "Endymion." "J. S. is perfectly right in regard to the slipshod Endymion. That it is so is no fault of mine. No! though it may sound a little paradoxical. It is as good as I had power to make it—by myself. Had I been nervous about its being a perfect piece, and with that view asked advice, and trembled over every page, it would not have been written; for it is not in my nature to fumble: I will write independently. I have written independently *without judgment*. I may write independently, and *with judgment* hereafter. The genius of poetry must work out its own salvation in a man. It cannot be matured by law and precept, but by sensation and watchfulness in itself." [42]

Yet for all the whim and mood and possible waywardness, no poet ever took his vocation more loftily or seriously, none ever felt more fully that work which the world will revere must be done in a spirit that the world can hardly understand. How noble, how pregnant, and how humble also is the advice to Shelley, whose methods were certainly far more erratic than those of Keats: "You, I am sure, will forgive me for sincerely remarking that you might curb your magnanimity, and be more of an artist, and load every rift of your subject with ore. The thought of such discipline must fall like cold chains upon you, who perhaps never sat with your wings furled for six months together. And is not this extraordinary talk for the writer of Endymion, whose mind was like a pack of scattered cards? I am picked up and sorted to a pip." [43]

Yet whether the work was carefully done or carelessly, there were plenty of difficulties about the doing of it. There were external difficulties such as every literary man is too familiar with; the interruptions, often well-intentioned and not unwelcome in themselves but disturbing to the full flow of inspiration; the necessary calls of business, the thousand little distractions, petty but irritating as the buzz of flies against a window-pane, if your attention gets fixed on them. As Keats himself puts it, "I carry all matters to an extreme; so that when I have any little vexation, it grows in five minutes into a theme for Sophocles." [44] It does not appear that the poet was unduly susceptible to these things. His work was done in all sorts of places and under conditions that cannot always have been wholly propitious. Yet he does at times complain that concentration was impossible: "In the way I am at present situated I have too many interruptions to a train of feeling to be able to write poetry." [45]

Again there were the external annoyances connected with literature itself, the brutality and stupidity of criticism. It was long ago recognized that any theory that Keats's death was caused by the attacks of *Blackwood* and *The Quarterly Review* is quite fantastic. The abuse of him had a large political element behind it, as he was no doubt well aware; there was plenty of praise as well as of abuse, and Keats's own temper was too manly to be ruinously or permanently affected by such wasp stings. Still they do fret and tease, and the repetition of them keeps one's mind on reviews and reviewers when it ought to be fixed on the production of work that no review could overthrow.

What gives these vexatious critics their power is that so much of oneself fights on their side. When one is clear in aim, confident in ability, secure in achievement, they may do their worst and one smiles at them. The trouble is the doubt in one's own heart that is worse than any critic. Keats was neither more diffident nor more hopeful than others; but he had his moments of despair in early days, and they kept returning to the end; despair because, after all, art was so great, the goal so high, life so short, and one's best efforts and best gifts so lamentably inadequate: "I have asked myself so often why I should be a poet more than other men, seeing how great a thing it is, . . . that at last the idea has grown so monstrously beyond my seeming power of attainment, that the other day I nearly consented with myself to drop into a Phaëthon." [46]

Yet the ardor was there, the mighty, divine, persistent ardor which would not allow difficulties of any kind to get the better of it—ever. Make these things trivial as they really are, wash and brush them off your spirit as you brush dust off your garments, and set to work oblivious of them. "Whenever I find myself growing vaporish, I rouse myself, wash, and put on a clean shirt, brush my hair and clothes, tie my shoestrings neatly, and in fact adonize as I were going out. Then, all clean and comfortable, I sit down to write. This I find the greatest relief." [47] So Buffon put on his finest garb when he prepared himself for a morning's work on his "Natural History." Then when the work gets into its splendor of spontaneous movement you forget clothes and difficulties altogether.

Intruding friends and enemies both vanish into the vague limbo of indifference, and nothing exists but that tardy pen which cannot with all its endeavor keep up with the rush of mighty thoughts and crowding fancies. "I have written this that you might see I have my share of the highest pleasures, and that though I may choose to pass my days alone, I shall be no solitary. . . . The only thing that can ever affect me personally for more than one short passing day, is any doubt about my powers for poetry: I seldom have any, and I look with hope to the nighing time when I shall have none. I am as happy as a man can be, . . . with the yearning passion I have for the beautiful, connected and made one with the ambition of my intellect." [48]

Here was the key of it all. Glory was very well, success was very well, but the one thing in life that counted was to create beauty for one's own perpetual delight and that of others. If Keats had died at seventy-five, instead of twenty-five, it may be that beauty would have seemed to him a less attainable, perhaps, alas, even a less adorable matter. Or he might have grown more secure in his worship as the years went on: there are a blessed few who do so. But in his life as it was, beauty was supreme,

from the first utterance of "Endymion," so hack-
neyed all over the world,

"A thing of beauty is a joy forever,"

to the proud conclusion of the "Grecian Urn,"

"Beauty is truth, truth beauty: that is all
Ye know on earth, and all ye need to know."

As he summed it up at the beginning of his career,
and kept it before him to the end: "I know no one
but you who can be fully sensible of the turmoil and
anxiety, the sacrifice of all what is called comfort,
the readiness to measure time by what is done and
to die in six hours could plans be brought to conclusions—the looking upon the sun, the moon, the
stars, the earth, and its contents—as materials to
form greater things, that is to say, ethereal things
—but here I am talking like a madman,—greater
things than our Creator himself made!" [49]

IV

But there was one spiritual element, one inter-
ruption if you like, that broke in upon this highly-
concentrated career and wrecked and shattered it
—and that was love. In the early days women

appear to have been to Keats like flowers and pictures. At times their tongues afflicted him. They seemed created to hand about the conventional chatter of society and it took a very pretty face to overcome this handicap: "She gave a remarkable prettiness to all those commonplaces which most women who talk must utter." [50] He complains that women want imagination, though he thinks it is a fortunate thing that they do.[51] When they are sweet and gay and simple he likes to while away an hour with them; but he fancies that they do not like his poetry, and fancies also that he understands the reason: "There is a tendency to class women in my books with roses and sweetmeats,—they never see themselves dominant." [52] In general he does not find himself at ease in their society: "When I am among women, I have evil thoughts, malice, spleen, I cannot speak, or be silent, I am full of suspicions and therefore listen to nothing, I am in a hurry to be gone." [53] As to love, before the full tempest struck him he was uncertain and mistrustful. Marriage might be very well for others—even one's brothers—commendable, necessary. Children, that is nephews and nieces, might be interesting, might be objects of affection. But for oneself it was a more doubt-

ful matter. There was work to be done—great
work, absorbing work, and it was a question
whether it could be done as well amid the agitations
of passion and domesticity. A fair woman might
be a delight to watch and study. When he meets
one such, he lets his imagination play about her in
a rapture which might easily be taken for personal
ecstasy. Not so. She is an exquisite work of art,
a dream, to be enjoyed and then forgotten. "You
will by this time think I am in love with her; so
before I go any further I will tell you I am not—
she kept me awake one night as a tune of Mozart's
might do." [54] And in general this love is to be
avoided: it is disturbing and dangerous. Did not
even Petrarch, the ideal lover, say: "It takes a
character of vast proportions to be equal to a wife
and literature both"? [55] No doubt Petrarch
knew. No: I will rebel, resist, keep away altogether: "Notwithstanding your happiness and your
recommendation, I hope I shall never marry. . . .
Instead of what I have described, there is a sub-
limity to welcome me home. The roaring of the
wind is my wife and the stars through the window-
pane are my children. . . . These things, combined
with the opinion I have of the generality of women,
who appear to me as children to whom I would

rather give a sugar plum than my time, form a barrier against matrimony which I rejoice in." [56]

Then Fanny Brawne appeared, and with a gradual, irresistible encroachment she absorbed his whole life. It is of course quite useless to look at the girl herself for any explanation of Keats's rapture. These things come from within, not from without, and are always inexplicable. Fanny appears to have been well enough but there is no evidence that she was an astounding beauty or that the world was mad about her. Explain it as you will, the chief sentence that she has left us in regard to her lover will always take care of her with posterity: "The kindest act would be to let him rest forever in the obscurity to which circumstances have condemned him." [57] A human being does not often have a chance to damn himself more completely than that. But to Keats she became at once the incarnation of the ideal, as they all do, and because the ideal was so high the incarnation was all the more enthralling. The absolute absorption of the whole thing shows in his earliest letters to her and continues to the end: "Ask yourself, my love, whether you are not very cruel to have so entrammeled me, so destroyed my freedom. Will you confess this in the letter you must write immediately and do all you can to console me in it? Make it rich as a draught of poppies to intoxicate me. Write the softest words and kiss them, that I may at least touch my lips where yours have been." [58]

The old glow of imagination shows here; but generally in the letters to Fanny the withering blast of passion dries up even the imaginative touch. They are simple, bare, direct; burn oftentimes with a rush of molten vigor but have no place for the brilliant play of fancy or the subtle elaboration of thought. Indeed, even in the other letters of the later days there is something of the same comparative barrenness. The winged spirit was chained, snared, enthralled, so that it could not soar with the old exuberant ecstasy.

Then the ruinous illness came and made it impossible for the engagement to ripen into marriage. For a long time hope dangled vainly before the lover's dying eyes. He would get better, he would enjoy her and life and poetry. There is no evidence that she was remiss in attention or unresponsive in tenderness. There was even talk of her marrying him and going to Italy to take care of him. But it was manifestly impossible and he went off alone, carrying her image with him everywhere with a fierce poignancy of intrusion which made his last hours burn with incomparable torture: "Oh, God! God! God! Everything I have in my trunks that reminds of her goes through me like a spear. The silk lining she put in my traveling cap scalds my head. My imagination is horribly vivid about her—I see her—I hear her. There is nothing in the world of sufficient interest to divert me from her a moment." [59]

The letters to Fanny Brawne have sometimes been regarded as unworthy of Keats and it has been urged that they should never have been published. To me this is quite incomprehensible. Keats's passion is as much a part of him as his genius. He was thoroughly human, his passion was thoroughly human, and the force with which it seized him was too thoroughly human to be in any way degrading. The agonies of fantastic jealousy, the torments and longings of absence and despair—who that has really loved will misinterpret them or feel that they disfigure genius or disgrace it?

It is true that in Keats's case they destroyed his genius by destroying him. It has been urged often enough that he was killed neither by criticism nor by love but by tuberculosis. No doubt both inherited predisposition and undue exposure hastened his end. But who can question that his body was burned up by his soul? If he had been content to live a fat, easy, Philistine life, taking the sweet of the world indolently as it came to him, tuberculosis might well enough have let him alone. A man with such a physique cannot live always in an atmosphere of high ecstasy as he did and not suffer for it. The devouring ardor and rapture of poetic creation strain the nerves enough. When added to them is such a love as Keats cherished for Fanny Brawne, there is too much encouragement to tuberculosis or anything else.

Love and glory killed him. The loss to the world has often been harped upon. Yet perhaps it was better to have left only those odes and sonnets and "Hyperion" than to have piled volume upon volume which no one would have time to read. As for himself, who can deplore his fate? He went believing in the endless possibility of love, the endless possibility of beauty, without finding as so many do that love satiates and beauty fades. It is true that he was not sure of his future fame; but would he have been more sure at eighty? Who ever is? And the thought of what he lost is less than of what he escaped.

That little, remote grave in Rome is infinitely

peaceful. The resting place of Shelley, further within the consecrated precincts, is somewhat dim and gloomy under the cold cypresses. But where Keats lies it is all sunshine: roses trail over it and violets linger. Surely those who have known most of his ardor, most of his aspiration, most of his hope, as they stand beside that tranquil corner cannot but sympathize with the words of a later poet:

> "And then we only ask some green retreat,
>   Some deep, sequestered nook by hill or shore,
> Where fame may never tempt our weary feet
>   To wander more.

> "A little resting-place, a quiet grave,
>   A sunny plot with violets overstrewn:
> No richer guerdon glory ever gave,
>   No sweeter boon."

VIII
GUSTAVE FLAUBERT

CHRONOLOGY

Gustave Flaubert
Born, Rouen, December 12, 1821
Traveled in Orient, 1849
Madame Bovary published, 1856
Salammbô published, 1862
L'Education Sentimentale published, 1869
La Tentation de Saint Antoine published, 1874
Died, Croisset, May 8, 1880

GUSTAVE FLAUBERT

I

Flaubert was born at Rouen in 1821 and died at Croisset near Rouen in 1880. The whole serious purpose of his existence was to interpret life in beautiful words. "My course," he says in 1852, "has never varied, from the time when I had to ask my nurse what letters to use to make the words of the phrases I invented, up to this evening, when the ink is drying on the erasures in my pages." [1] He might have said the same twenty-five years later. It is true that he did not settle to systematic work very early. His father was a physician and he himself was bred to the law. But he never liked it and never practiced. He had a moderate but sufficient patrimony, and at twenty-five he set himself to literature as a business, an enormously engrossing, destroying business, and practically never left it.

At the same time no one understood better than

243

Flaubert that literature is based on life and cannot exist a moment without it. More than that, he had a natural zest for living, entered into pleasures and pains, both his own and others', with extraordinary keenness and intensity. He could snatch the bloom off a bit of passion and brood on it for years: "If I have arrived at a certain knowledge of life, it is by having lived little in the ordinary sense of the word; for I have eaten little, but ruminated much." [2] Words were absorbing, delightful to him: they were his instruments, his tools, full of endless revelation and charm; but back of words were always things, obscure, uncertain, tormenting you, teasing you, holding you, and making you and the words do their bidding.

Before literature got hold of him completely, he went out into the world with an enthusiastic ardor for travel. The Orient fascinated his rich and oriental imagination and for over a year he wandered through the picturesque East. Such voyaging then meant rough experiences; but this was nothing to Flaubert. He had a superb physique, was a great, blonde, Norman giant, made for mad adventures and robust toil. His nerves were highstrung and sensitive and when he abused them by reckless disregard of hygiene they finally played

him false. But he bullied them and mastered them
at all times. When he was a child he was timid and
full of fears. But he went after peril and faced it
down, did wild things for the pure discipline of it,
"all for the sake of becoming brave, and I have become so."[3] Therefore he laughed at the toils
and annoyances and hardships of travel, and even
enjoyed them. "I am a Barbarian," he says of his
physical constitution: "I have their muscular
apathy, their nervous languors, their green eyes,
and their vast stature."[4]

In the East he enjoyed everything. Nature enchanted him, the wide spaces, the tropical odors,
the monotony of the desert, the blaze of the unbroken sun, the calm splendor of the stars. That
wealth of imaginative suggestion which enriches his
letters more than those of any one, unless Keats,
is all expended upon depicting and interpreting
this charm of the Orient: the color, the solitude, the
stinging, penetrating, exotic qualities of sound, and
even more the oppression and exhilaration of
silence. He carried it all home in his heart and
dreamed of it for years. Again and again in his
later correspondence there peeps out some memory
of those old remote wanderings, and they gave him
ample background for the poetry of *Salammbô* and

Saint-Antoine. Yet he was well aware that the nature that really counts for us is that we have grown up with. The picturesque of far countries is well enough to remember; but what enters into the tissue of our lives is the woods and fields we have roamed in childhood, the simple flowers and sounds and lights of home. And he reminds us of the profound truth: "It is only commonplaces and well-known countries that have inexhaustible beauty." [5]

If the landscape of the Orient appealed to him, perhaps humanity appealed to him even more. The intense vivid quickness of his response to the external world, in spite of superficial cynicism, appears in a careless phrase of his later years: "If one were to derange one's habits for every thing that is worth seeing, one would not stay still a minute in an existence of a century." [6] His younger heart did not care to stay still, and his eyes and ears feasted on all that Eastern tumult of passion and movement and color and life.

But this was play. After it he went home and settled down and worked—worked with a dogged, persistent, devouring ardor which few literary men or any other kind of men have ever surpassed. He sat at his desk and stuck there; allowed no diversion,

no reasonable, necessary exercise, hardly a duty
even to distract him from it. There were moments
when nature rebelled, when he had to relax and give
up: "I am going to eat, smoke, yawn in the sun,
above all sleep. I sometimes have vast impulses
to sleep for days on end." [7] But these were only
moments. In the main it was one steady, prolonged, terrific effort, towards a definite aim. For
his work was not done, as is that of some authors,
with a golden outflow of spontaneous ease. The
even, rapid, unfailing production of a Scott or a
Sand or a Trollope was incomprehensible to him.
He finds no fault with this; on the contrary, envies
it: "It is trying to see how the great men get their
effects easily, without the effort of art." [8] But
such achievement is not for him. With all his
enormous labor he cannot produce more than a half
dozen small books in thirty years. A sentence
sometimes costs him hours, even days of toil. A
page has to be re-written and re-cast and re-con-
ceived until it is finally accepted as perfect, if it
ever is. "I do not know where this difficulty of
finding the right word will end; I am not inspired,
very far from it." [9] Again, "I have now spent
three days in making two corrections, which will not

come: the whole day Monday, and Tuesday also, were passed in the search for two lines." [10]

Work done so slowly of course implies immense difficulty in the doing. You may insist as much as you like that obstinacy will overcome all difficulties,[11] the difficulties are there, just the same, sometimes mountainous and almost insuperable. The external difficulties are bad enough, the interruptions, the distractions—petty in themselves but intolerable when the nerves are fretted and strained. People will intrude their chatter and their irrelevance and their questions, till at length the writer cries in despair, "To accomplish anything I must have the impossibility of being disturbed, even if I wished it." [12] Far slighter things than the intrusion of people will set one's thoughts a-dancing, scatter concentration almost irrecoverably: "a windowshade askew, a fly that buzzes, the noise of a cart passing, and my fancy is off at once." [13] But even with perfect quiet, even in the dim seclusion of midnight with the curtains drawn and the lamp singing monotonously, there are still the obstacles from within, inexplicable but hampering, harassing, blocking. The words will not put themselves together, the phrases will not get their music, the incidents and the people are all criss-cross and out of place. "I lead a harsh life, barren of all outward delight, and in which I have nothing to sustain me but a sort of enduring rage, which sometimes weeps for impotence, but persists forever. . . . Sometimes when I find myself empty, when expression simply refuses to come, when, after having scribbled long pages, I discover that I have not made one single perfect phrase, I fall upon my divan and lie there stupefied in a smother of fatigue and disgust." [14]

So, often there come waves of vast discouragement and despair. Art is so difficult, so enormously difficult, so impossible. One sees the beauty achieved by others but somehow one cannot oneself attain it, at least not as one wishes. "Oh, how often I have fallen back to earth, my nails bleeding, my sides bruised, my head swimming, after having tried to climb straight up this marble wall!" [15] And at times the despair is so dense, so prostrating that one is tempted to give up altogether, leave art to others, enjoy and seek to create no longer. "I said to myself, 'is art worth so much vexation? . . . Of what use are such passionate sacrifices merely to end in mediocrity?'" [16]

But the born writer cannot give up, never gives up. No matter how the troubles swarm, he grits his teeth, perhaps bows for the moment, but is at work again before you know it—grimly determined to deserve success, whether he achieves it or not. And then, suddenly from one knows not where, there come the hours of delight when all goes as it should, when the golden words slip easily into their places and the rich music of the phrase sounds more gloriously in your own ears than perhaps it ever will in any others. And even as you feel it, you analyze it; but you feel it just the same: "I was moved myself, I enjoyed deliciously both the emotion of the subject and of the phrase which rendered it and the satisfaction of having found that phrase. At least I believe there were all these elements in my feeling, in which no doubt the strain and quiver of the nerves had an important place. But there was more in it than mere nerves, an ecstasy in which the physical element is nothing, which passes even virtue in spiritual beauty, because it is so independent of everything personal, of every human relation." [17] And so the days and the hours and the years were absorbed in work.

II

But life could not be all work, even with this indefatigable worker. Although the voyaging of

GUSTAVE FLAUBERT

youth was over, one could not shut oneself up entirely and forget the world. One's work would be the worse for such a seclusion, if one's heart were not. It was easy to say, "as for us, living is not our business; all we need think of personally is not to suffer." [18]

But at least you had to meet humanity, if you did not live with it; to touch men and watch them and talk with them and deal with them, however impatient you might be to get back to pen and ink.

And Flaubert did all these things, did them intelligently if reluctantly, and perhaps not always reluctantly if the truth were known. Business relations indeed he hated, was apparently inept and indifferent in matters of money, though he was always exact and conscientious. And he had that frugality which enabled him to have cash for his own needs and for his friends', when it was required. How charming is his simple offer to lend to his adored George Sand, with whom money was always pouring in and pouring out, she could not tell how. [19]

In the more intimate connections of life Flaubert appears thoroughly attractive. As he had neither wife nor child of his own, all his real depth of affection was expended upon his relatives, and he cherished them with singular tenderness. It is true that they sometimes interrupted him and bothered him, true that his theory was all against them: "The born poet is for me a priest: as soon as he puts on the priestly garment, he should quit his family forever." [20] He quotes with delightful envy, but also with some appreciation of its significance, the admirable sentence in which his mother ventured to criticize his mode of life: "The rage for phrases has withered up your heart." [21] Yet he worshiped his mother and made every possible effort and sacrifice for her. Of his dead sister he says, "With her I buried much of my ambition, almost every desire of earthly glory: I had brought her up, she had a firm and delicate soul which was all my joy." [22] And his tenderness for his niece shows both in his letters to her and in all her words about him.

But for humanity at large he cannot be said to have had much regard. It is evident that he did not move easily among strangers, did not open himself to them either to give or to receive. "It appears," he says, "that when I have on evening clothes I am no longer the same. It is certain that I am then wearing a disguise, and my physiognomy and my manners must show the effect of it: the

exterior does so influence the interior." [23] At
any rate, he did not have the intense impulse that
draws men to their fellows whether they are immediately sympathetic or not, the pleasure in
human contact just because it is human. On the
contrary, he shrank, turned away, or if he looked, it
was rather to emphasize the tedious and offensive
sides. Perhaps he did not enough allow for the
tendency to reduce any crowd to its lowest and most
conspicuous elements. The *bourgeois,* the average,
ordinary man with his ordinary thoughts and ordinary passions and ordinary laughter irritated him.
When he has to go to a funeral he rebels, not because mortality troubles him but "because the contemplation of the greater part of my fellows grows
more and more odious to me, nervously speaking." [24] And this feeling increases until he insists that they are not his fellows, for good or for
evil are altogether different: "I detest my fellow-
men and do not admit that I am akin to them: I
am sure that men are no more brothers than the
leaves in the woods are alike: they suffer in common, that is all." [25]

Nevertheless, in spite of this appearance of a
misanthropy as bitter as Swift's, there is no question but that Flaubert could be a charming com-

panion when he pleased. Those who knew him intimately all testify to his frankness, his cordiality, his boisterous, rollicking spirits, his splendid abundance of rich and entertaining talk. At the Magny dinners, so fully described in the Goncourt *Journal*, still more in the later, more intimate reunions with Goncourt, Zola, Daudet, Turgenev, he appears with a singular and attractive abandon, pouring out his own experiences and listening to those of others with equal zest.

And however he detested humanity in general, he was a most devoted, affectionate, and self-sacrificing friend. His letters are full not only of warm tenderness but of constant sympathetic inquiry and solicitude. His attachment to the memory of the poet Bouilhet and his effort to preserve and cherish it are most touching and winning. And there is no sweeter or more charming monument of friendship than the long-continued correspondence between him and George Sand. When they became acquainted, Madame Sand was well past the passionate impulses of her youth, and she was so much older that she could treat Flaubert almost as a son. But there are in existence few exchanges of letters between two geniuses each so rarely gifted and at the same time so strongly contrasted with each other. And the contrast did not prevent their understanding and above all loving each other with a constant depth of tenderness. Though George Sand represented everything in art most different from Flaubert's own achievement and ideal, he was able to appreciate fully the nobility and largeness of her character, and no one understood better than she the passionate contradictions which at once tormented and sustained his lofty effort.

Above all, she urged that his misanthropy was a pose, that he insisted upon hardening his heart and rebelling against all his gentler impulses, but that really his inner nature was all sympathy and kindness, and it is hard to read his letters carefully and not agree with her. He might repeat as much as he pleased, "I have little sensibility for collective misfortunes. Nobody pities my miseries; why should I trouble myself about those of others? I return humanity what it gives me, *indifference*." [26] But the wide pity peeps through, nevertheless: "I have had compassion for many things which ordinarily sensitive people do not trouble themselves about." [27] And one feels the intimate truth of George Sand's assertion: "You try to shut up an overflowing spirit in a jail, to make wilful misanthropy out of a tender and in-dulgent heart—but you will never succeed." [28]

The truth is, the man's intelligence and his emo-tions were at war, as so often happens in this fight-ing world. The emotions were all pity for human folly and incompetence and, if you like, baseness. But the uncompromising intelligence demanded al-ways that life should be other than it is. He was a thorough-going idealist and, as with so many of that type, the idealism soured into pessimism be-cause it could never be satisfied. The deepest pes-simism does not spring from mere negation, still less from a fat and slothful materialism, which is apt to enjoy its senses and let the world go: the saddest pessimist, whether Madame du Deffand or Flaubert, is one who asks too much of life and of the living; one whose ideal is so high, whose con-ception of what men should be, of what men might be is so noble that the sordid reality, as it creeps upon the dull and muddy earth, breeds nothing but perpetual disappointment and despair. Human souls might be glorious in hope, in aspiration, in love, even in actual achievement, and they are—what they are.

So you turn away sadly into the "ivory tower," where ideal thought and beauty dwell, there to weave dreams and visions with exquisite words and phrases that cannot die. Unfortunately, after all, the only stuff your dreams are made of, or ever can be, is just this weak, stumbling, groping, deplorable humanity, which you reject and despise. And more unfortunately still, when you are constituted like Flaubert, what you emphasize in your dream-weaving is the intellectual, not the emotional part of you. Therefore Flaubert's art, great and exquisite as it is, is bitter when it should not have been and need not have been. All through his novels there is the finest, the subtlest, the profoundest observation of life. But though he insisted that it was abstract, detached, impersonal, the stamp of his own bitter disillusion is upon it. So with his characters. They are done with a depth and power that make it impossible to forget them: Madame Bovary herself, the incomparable Homais, Jacques Arnoux; those strange twins of the world's irony, Bouvard and Pécuchet. But surely there are some men and women who are lovable; only not in the novels of Flaubert. It may be that George Sand saturated her books with the milk of human kindness; yet a drop or two would not have damaged those of her greater friend, no matter how much he would have resented it.

III

But again you could not work at phrases or dream creatures all the time whether they were ugly or beautiful. Fortunately there was the world of thought and reflection to distract you as well as the world of humanity. What marks Flaubert in this, as in everything, is that he was passionate and intense. There was no casual interest, no light or flippant curiosity for him. Anything that was worth attention at all was worth profound attention, worth loving or hating with all possible energy. "The moment I cease to be indignant, I shall fall flat, like a puppet when you take away the support." [29] It is this vivid intensity which makes the purely humorous attitude, of Lamb for instance, as utterly impossible for Flaubert as for Voltaire. The former bewails his lack in this respect. He insists that he sees the comic side of things, and in a sense he does. He envies the broad, sweet, universal laughter of Rabelais and Cervantes, and wishes he could get something of it into his work. Vain effort! You cannot smile kindly and tolerantly when you are full of fierce loving or hating. A broad burlesque, a violent buffoonery, Flaubert sometimes has. Pure comedy he has not.

As regards the subjects of thinking, it would not be expected that he would have much sympathy with applied thought in practical matters. The compromises necessary to run the daily machinery of life were irritating, incomprehensible to him. Action in the sense of the concrete managing of the world's affairs, did not tempt him in the slightest. At worst it was tainted with base and sordid motives. At best it was often incomplete and often futile. The fact that the world's work must be done did not greatly impress him. Why must it be done? Let all go to ruin, if necessary: things would not be likely to be much worse than they are now. Anyway, what would it matter to Sirius? Far better that a thing should not be done at all than be bungled and botched and left a pitiful spectacle of imperfection for fools to mock at and the wise to sigh over. The Second Empire, under which he came to manhood, disgusted him. But the Republic that followed it was even worse and more contemptible. And in general his attitude was: "As for me, I execrate all that is obligatory, all law, all government, all rule. Who art thou, O Society, that thou shouldst *force* me to anything whatever? What god has made thee my master?" [30]

The man found himself more at ease in abstract thinking. Here he could give his splendid ardor full rein without stumbling over the inconvenient obstacles of fact. When he felt that he could let his work go he liked to surge out into great thoughts; to toss and tumble the problems of the universe with swift, burning, fearless fingers; to set his solid, Norman, barbarian shoulder to upheaving old theories and dull secure beliefs, regardless of what might come in place of them. He wanted to read everything, to think everything, to know everything, though his restless activity would have been in despair if anything could have been really known. "I am thirsty for long studies and fierce labors." [31] He read the fathers of the Latin Church. He read the vast series of German philosophers. He tore the world to pieces with his penetrating analysis: "The deplorable mania of analysis exhausts me. I doubt everything, even doubt itself." [32] Yet so essentially dynamic and constructive was his temperament that the doubt was not merely sceptical but always fruitful, stimulating, full of suggestion and development. Like Keats he protested against systems, but only in behalf of truth. "Conclusion seems to me, for the most part, an act of folly." [33] Let reason rove, and follow its leading fearlessly into all sorts of strange regions, always with wonder and delight.

So with religion. Flaubert was never a mocking sceptic, never could have been. Life in all its aspects was too earnest, too serious. You must find the key to it even if it never could be found. He deplored the lack of religion in men like Musset: *"You cannot live without religion.* That sort of people have none whatever, no compass, no object; they float from day to day, torn by all the passions and all the vanities of the passing hour." [34] And he had a kind of tenderness for the forms of positive faith. He reads the Bible devotedly. "For three years I read it every evening before going to sleep. At the very first free moment I have I am going to begin again." [35] He has strange spiritual yearnings and might have been a mystic if he had not been an author: "If it were not for the love of form, I should perhaps have been an ardent mystic. My attacks of nerves are nothing but involuntary cataclysms of ideas and images: the psychic element then gets away with me and consciousness disappears with all immediate sensation of life." [36] Yet with religion as with other things there is always the dread of fixation, of dogmatism, and the feeling that dogmatism means death. Make your belief as you go, then let your belief make you, and so sweep on into the infinite in a perpetual joyous process of evolution and growth. "Light people, shallow people, presumptuous and eager spirits want conclusions in everything: they seek the object of life and the dimensions of the infinite. They take in their poor little hands a bit of sand and they say to the Ocean: 'I am going to count the grains on all your shores.' But as the grains slip through their fingers and the count is wearying, they tremble and weep. Do you know the only thing to be done on that vast shore? You must either kneel or stroll. I stroll." [37]

But if Flaubert put passion into thinking about God and the universe generally, he put it most of all into thinking about art and beauty, since these matters came so nearly home to himself. He was not particularly interested in sculpture or painting, yet the note of enthusiasm before a bit of ruined statue at Athens rings with the ecstasy with which all loveliness affected him: "How gladly would I have fallen upon my knees before it, with my hands crossed in devotion . . . a little more, and I should have prayed." [38]   And when he approaches the masters of literature his ardor is unbounded. Shakespeare? He buries himself in Shakespeare: common things and common thoughts are lost in that wilderness of beauty. Don Quixote? He has lived with Don Quixote from a child, has adored him always. And be it noted that there was a certain noble affinity between the Don and Flaubert himself: the ideal hope, the ideal struggle, the ideal passion for shattering the noisy, futile windmills of the world. In connection with these works of perfect or aspiring art, Flaubert pours out to his correspondents all sorts of theories and suggestions and comments on the nature and object of art itself. Here again, as with philosophy and religion, there is no effort at consistent or systematic thinking. Creeds and dogmas are as cold and lifeless, as misleading and fatal, in matters of beauty as in matters of pure truth. Feel, seek, aspire, enjoy, above all labor with all the power that is in you. Leave the systems to those who know little about enjoyment and nothing about creation. It is evident enough that Flaubert's ideas and sayings on these things are confused, incoherent, often incompatible. But no one can resist the vigor and

263

the splendor of them. They are the outpouring of
a spirit itself splendidly creative and dashing off
sparks of dazzling illumination as it goes.

Of course in all the comment and analysis he
is thinking of his own creation. How could it be
otherwise? He explains and dissects his own artistic
practice with constant curiosity and anxiety. To
produce beauty, immortal beauty, but how? That
is the point. And it cannot be denied that by
nature and temperament his attention is mainly
fixed upon detail, as indeed he himself admits. He
labors with his plan, he tries to make a large con-
ception, does make it. Then he spends months
and years on the structure of sentences, and somehow the general movement is more or less obscured
and effaced. He is enchanted with rhythm, seeks
strange and subtle effects of haunting music, con-
trasts and correspondences, sometimes hidden from
all ears but his, yet again enthralling any reader
for whom verbal magic has charm. He works over
words, toils to make them yield all their secrets,
to find the one perfect expression which can alone
convey the weight of meaning with which his spirit
aches to burden it. For note that always with
Flaubert, style is fundamentally and eternally one
with thought. It is no mere varnish, no superficial

ornament. It is simply the best, final, perfect way of saying what you have to say. If you have nothing to say, style is nothing, there can be none. He laughs at the people who call it a garment. "No, no! Form is the very flesh of thought, as thought is the soul of life: the larger the muscles of your chest are, the greater the ease with which you breathe." [39] And so all this ardor for beauty is but ardor for the expression of life. Life is the gross, crude substance; but it is all the substance, and art is merely the means of taking life, in its ugliness, its crudeness, its grossness, and making it eternal and worthy to be eternal, by the transmuting, transfiguring glory of creative loveliness. Poetry is not merely moonshine and flowers: "we must get it out of anything whatever; for it is to be found anywhere and in all things." [40] If the artist is to achieve this, he must sink himself, must be consecrated, must be a priest of the high altar of the muses. His own narrow, feeble personality must be left out and not allowed to act as an obscuring veil between the grosser stuff of life and the celestial radiance of beauty.

Difficult and in some respects incomprehensible as these theorizings may be, one must take them into account in understanding the realism which produced *Madame Bovary* and *L'Education Senti-mentale*. It was a matter of principle with Flaubert to take the commonest material, the everyday wear and drag of plain, prosaic, ugly life and show that the highest beauty could be made out of it? Immoral? Was life immoral? Was truth immoral? Be true and your art could not be immoral. Only keep your poor petty personality, your own trivial, narrow emotions out of the matter; make your work impersonal and eternal, and it would be as moral as God. Unfortunately we have already seen that what Flaubert considered the personal part of him was his tenderness, his sympathy, all his human and kindly impulses. The impersonal was his intellect. And his intellect was idealistic—it tried poor humanity by an ideal standard and condemned it. Hence his intellect was cruel. So too was his work.

Yet it is most curious to see how in the splendid spontaneity of his letters, written without curious labor or effort to make every detail perfect, the whole man shines forth in instinctive rebellion against this realistic work that he was doing so completely on a theory. He loved romance, he loved color, he loved poetry, he loved dreams. In the strange visions of *Salammbô* and *Saint-Antoine* he indulged these ardors to some extent. But even here the intellect, the bitterness, the analysis trammeled him. There was a cruel conflict in his spirit always, and no labor, no thought, no theorizing sufficed to reconcile or overcome it. He could not somehow attain the serenity of the greatest masters, could not achieve the light and splendor and glory for which he so passionately longed. Scores of passages in the letters suggest the longing, as this on the reveries of his youth: "Between the world and me existed I know not what screen of stained glass, stained yellow, with rays of fire and arabesques of gold, so that all things were reflected on my soul as on the pavement of a sanctuary, embellished, transfigured, yet melancholy, and only what was beautiful found place there, in dreams more majestic and more richly garmented than cardinals in purple robes. Ah, what shudderings of proud delight, what hymns, what a delicious odor of incense exhaling from a thousand caskets, always opened wide! When I am old, I will write all this, and it will warm my heart. I will do as those do who, before setting out upon a long journey, visit the graves of their beloved dead. I, before I die, will revisit my dreams." [41]

IV

This intense, passionate, high-wrought, imaginative temperament of Flaubert constantly recalls Keats, and makes one ask how love, which played such havoc with Keats's imagination, affected Flaubert. It is evident that his general attitude toward women was much the same as that of Keats: they were exquisite toys to trifle with, but somewhat alien from the serious purpose of life, in Enobarbus's phrase: "though it were pity to cast them away for nothing, as between them and a great cause, they should be esteemed nothing." Flaubert's comments on the sex at large, on their sentiments and their interests, are too apt to be marked with that fierce and acrid veracity which women find so peculiarly distasteful. "The heart, the heart, the poor heart, the kindly heart, the charming heart with its eternal graces, is always there, even with the most intelligent and the greatest." [42] To which should be added the cruel corollary from another letter: "Women who mistake their senses for their heart." [43]

As for marriage and children and domestic life, these things are quite left out of Flaubert's scheme of existence. They may be all very well for the

268

bourgeois, necessary and suitable. For the artist they hardly count. Even the praise of marriage treats it from an ideal point of view which amounts to satire: "I believe, like the pariah of Bernardin de Saint-Perre, that happiness is to be found with a good woman. The difficulty is to come across her, and to be oneself a good man, a double and quite appalling preliminary." [44] Children Flaubert rarely if ever mentions. No doubt he loved those near to him and did what he could for them, as evidently for his niece; but there is nothing of Victor Hugo's or Swinburne's adoration.

Yet it was impossible that such an ardent soul should not understand and to some extent cherish ideal passions, no matter how much analysis might undermine and destroy them. In his extreme youth there was a certain lady at Trouville who took possession of his whole being till her image mastered and involved years of his life: "I loved one woman from the time I was fourteen till I was twenty, without ever touching her; and for three years afterward I never gave sex a thought. For a time I believed that it would be so till I died, and I thanked God for it." [45] But the way in which love shows itself most with that literary temperament is in the caressing dreams of memory, and the passages in which Flaubert elaborates and dwells upon these have extraordinary vividness: "I recall the spasms that shook me, the depths of grief, the strange longings like gusts hissing through a vessel's cordage, and the vast vague desires whirling in the black void, like gulls in the fury of tempest."[46] Or again he has this subtle and profound definition of melancholy: "No! No! Days of gaiety, have too, too sad tomorrows: and melancholy is nothing but a past which does not know itself." [47]

The only later love affair that seems to have taken deep hold upon Flaubert's life is that recorded for us in the long series of letters to Madame X (Louise Colet), covering (with a considerable break) the years from 1846 to 1854. If this love had no other significance, it would have immortal value in having produced these letters; for there are none in the world, except a few of Keats, that can pretend to rival them in height and depth of imaginative intensity and beauty. Flaubert pours out his whole life and thought, his whole ambition and effort and despair, in these wonderful pages, with the speed and abandon which he so carefully and tragically kept out of his books. As for love, well, it must be admitted that he was a singular lover. He tries his best, lashes his sides to achieve the ideal which perhaps no one but him could have conceived or aimed at. Yet the damnable analysis will enter in and show its lurking serpent head everywhere. This is the best he can do, and you see what it amounts to: "None of those I have actually loved has been worth you, and I doubt if those I have longed for would have been worth you either. I sometimes try to imagine your face when you have grown old, and it seems to me that I shall love you quite as much or even more." [48] And the analysis often takes more dubious and destructive forms than this: "Men, in fact, always want to make themselves beloved even when they do not love, and if I have sometimes wished that you loved me less, it was in the moments when I loved you most, when I saw you suffering on my account." [49] Which is complicated, to say the least of it.

The truth was that love was doubtful as an ideal and extremely difficult in the actual practice. It was a craving to get fulfillment outside oneself, and this was weakness, after all: "For it is a corruption not to be sufficient unto oneself." [50] At any rate, love was difficult for him: he was not made for it or, however it might have been in young days at Trouville, at thirty he was past the age of ecstasy.

"A man like me, grown old in all the excesses of solitude, ready to collapse with nervous strain, torn with dead, trampled passions, full of uncertainty without and even within, is not the one you should have loved." [51] Love is too violent, tumultuous, full of conflict and despair; he does not know what to make of it or to do with it: "Such is my pitiable nature: if you did not love me, I should die; you love me, and I write and beg you to cease loving. . . . Yet, don't, don't curse me: I shall have loved you enormously before I love you no longer." [52]

But there was no use talking; the demands of this insatiable eternal feminine were too exacting, were impossible. He wrote to her, he thought of her, he loved her, what did she want more? His whole self? My God! He couldn't give it: no man could who had a self worth giving. Jealous? What was she jealous of? The old lips he had kissed, the old thoughts he had flung away? He could not dig them up and tear them in pieces: why not let them rest? He gave her what he could, all he could, more than he could. It was poor enough but it was all: why not be content? "I love you as I can, not enough, I know it, I know it. But, my God! whose is the fault?" [53]

Then there was his art. After all, his art was his

life and the rest was mere distraction; at least he could give it only the leavings, however unworthy. "How can you expect that a man bruised and crushed by art as I am, perpetually craving an ideal that he can never attain . . . should love with a heart of twenty years and should have that ingenuousness which is the supreme charm of all passion?" [54] He urges her to remember that there is something in life more than enjoyment, more than love even, "something that sings through everything, no matter whether one stops one's ears, or gives one's whole soul to listening to it, something to which the merely *contingent* is of no account, and which has the nature of the angels, who require no mortal nourishment: I mean, the ideal." [55] But she was a woman and the ideal seemed cold to her, chilly and far away, especially as it was his ideal, not hers. And the end was what might be expected. What she felt we shall never know. But he, after due protest and regret, shut himself into that tower of ivory and made phrases for twelve hours a day with more than a lover's ardor, and forgot.

And one asks, as usual rather vainly, why he did it? Was it the desire of success, fame, applause, to flutter through the mouths of men? Yet

Flaubert joins the almost unanimous chorus of artists who vociferate loudly that they do not care for this. It is rare indeed that one meets the straightforward honesty of the Goncourts' avowal: "Our disease at bottom is literary ambition, insatiable and embittered, the perpetual irritation of the vanity of letters, when the newspaper that does not speak of you wounds you, and that which speaks of others drives you to despair." [56] With Flaubert there is no such frankness as this. He works apart, indifferent, and the rapture or railing of the crowd is not supposed to affect him.

All the same, the criticisms do prick, and the scorn and the abuse, when one knows that one is doing one's best. To work ten years with unselfish devotion on a masterpiece and then publish it and be haled into the police court as an enemy of morality is intensely disagreeable, however one may despise the opinions of men. The "Père Beuve" is a great critic, but when he ventures to pick flaws in *Salammbô* it is hard to think of his greatness or his criticism with equanimity. And again one goes on working, gives up life and love for it, in one's later years turns out phrases that appear to ring with a strange magic such as no ear or heart can resist—and the public is callous, or even mocking, and the dim echo of it all in an ivory tower is not soothing to nerves always stretched to tortured tautness by abnormal effort.

No, glory is not indifferent, and the verdict of readers must be considered, as well as one's own. In Flaubert's youthful days there is a fairly frank word about it: "I do not despise glory. . . . My heart has beaten at the word perhaps more passionately than most hearts." [57] And even toward the end he permitted himself to be fooled by the thought of it, as Henry James was, into that most betwitching, ensnaring, deluding, defrauding of all seductions for the purely literary man—the theatre. And if he did not know the sweet of glory in this line, he at least tasted the intensity of bitterness and disappointment.

Yet after all, glory was a small part of it, and what really counted, as with Keats, was the pure ecstasy of creating beauty, of feeling these strange, mysterious, magical phrases emanate in their satisfying perfection from depths of your being that you did not know and could not understand. There was toil about it, torture about it; but there was rapture about it also, beyond the rapture of worldly success, beyond the rapture of contented and eternally discontented love. Joy was not the word, happiness was not the word: it was rather the mystic's ecstasy of self-achieving, self-dissolving oblivion.

And so, after all these months and years of enormous, exhausting labor, shattering the nerves and withering up the heart, Flaubert left behind him his half-dozen books which posterity will prize among its treasures. Yet curiously enough, the very effort of perfection that he lavished upon them seems to make the imperfections stand out all the more. On the other hand, his letters, which presumably he did not work over at all, and which simply welled up from the profoundest depths of his passionate soul, will always remain one of the richest and finest expressions of such a soul that the world has ever seen. And still more curiously, it was the extreme endeavor of his art to be objective and impersonal, to render life without the intrusion of his own emotions and experiences; yet the part of his work that touches us most is the intense utterance of himself. *Madame Bovary* is the triumph of the art, but the letters are the triumph of the artist.

IX
EDWARD FITZGERALD

CHRONOLOGY

Edward Fitzgerald

Born, Bredfield House, Suffolk, March 31, 1809

At Cambridge, 1826-1830

Married Miss Barton, 1856

Translation of the *Rubáiyát* of Omar Khayyám published, 1859

Bought Little Grange, Woodbridge, 1864

Died, Merton, Norfolk, June 14, 1883

EDWARD FITZGERALD

I

WHAT strikes us in America first, and perhaps most, in a life like that of Edward Fitzgerald is the utter idleness. In spite of the growth of wealth and luxury, an American youth, no matter what his means or position, generally expects to get educated and then go out and do something in the world, for his own self-respect if not for the benefit of others. Fitzgerald was born in 1809, spent some years of his childhood in France, was educated at King Edward the Sixth's School at Bury St. Edmunds and at Cambridge. Then, until 1883, he walked a little, talked a little, thought a little, scribbled a little as he would have said himself, smoked a great deal, and died.

Fitzgerald's idleness is made especially interesting and puzzling by the feeling of splendid powers and abilities which might have done great things, anything, and did not. He was as modest a man as ever lived. How charming is the humble comparison of himself with his friend Tennyson: "Perhaps I have received some benefit in the now more distinct consciousness of my dwarfishness." [1] Yet the more you know of him, the more you perceive a certain meaning in the self-rallying sentence: "I am of that superior race of men, that are quite content to hear themselves talk, and read their own writing." [2] He was superior. Yet he did nothing.

He had health sufficient, perhaps not robust in later years; perhaps, even in earlier, a little too much the subject of attention from the mere idleness, but health sufficient to have done great work in the world. He congratulates himself on his freedom from nerves: "Cambridge looked very ghastly, and the hard-reading, pale, dwindled students walking along the Observatory road looked as if they were only fit to have their necks wrung. I scorn my nerveless carcase more and more every day." [3] He had admirable intellectual gifts, broad understanding, tolerant judgment, the richness of human sympathy which is so valuable in the management of men. He had equal moral qualities: courage, vigor, energy. He often deplores the absence of these things, but it is perfectly evident that all he needed was an adequate occasion to call them out. Yet he did nothing.

And all the time you feel that he despised indolence and loved and admired a life of great, wide action, which would move the world, and stir it, and lift it. He has no patience with daintiness, or girlishness, or pretty casual trifles. With what enthusiasm does he commend the early, homely education of Carlyle: "Ah, it is from such training that strength comes, not from luxurious fare, easy chairs, cigars, Pall Mall Clubs, etc." [4] What appeals to him, what rouses him is heroic achievement. He reads Thucydides and the battles set him on fire. "It came upon me *come stella in ciel,*' when, in the account of the taking of Amphipolis, Thucydides, 'who wrote down these things,' comes with seven ships to the rescue. Fancy old Hallam sticking to his gun at a Martello tower. This was the way to write well." [5] And it was the way to live well, and it was the way he was born to live. Yet he did nothing.

Somehow the sense of Fitzgerald's wasted ability overcomes one most in connection with the sea. He loved the sea always, loved to live near it, loved sea things and sea people: "I always like seafaring people; and go now every day almost on the water." [6] He owned boats and sailed them and felt an almost personal affection for them. He loved to dream on the ocean, and I am sure he would have liked to fight on it. Perhaps he was born out of time and missed his chance by fate as well as by perversity. "It is not my talent to take the tide at its flow; and so all goes to worse than waste." [7] It may have been his misfortune also. And I can imagine him really at home in the old days, with Drake and Blake and Raleigh, fighting tempests, fighting Spaniards, sailing with rapture out into the great unknown, and desperately busy instead of drifting through the nineteenth century in idleness.

What shows this sea passion and action more than anything else is his love and praise of the manly, sturdy sea captain who sailed Fitzgerald's ship and served to embody his ideal of an active, heroic life. This man did not talk, he did things. This man came into a house on shore and seemed to fill it and overflow it. But put him on shipboard and he had a magnificent natural dignity and was adequate to the storm. How significant is Fitzgerald's grouping of him with Tennyson and Thackeray. "When Tennyson was with me, whose portrait hangs in my house in company with those of Thackeray and this man (the three greatest men I have known), I thought that both Tennyson and Thackeray were inferior to him in respect of thinking of themselves. . . . 'You know,' said Scott to Lockhart, 'that I don't care a curse about what I write,' and one sees he did not." [8]

I know nothing that brings out more fully the suggestion of repressed energy, of repressed life in Fitzgerald than the admirable description of his nocturnal restlessness: "So, as I can't read at night, and my reader does not come till eight, I stride up and down a sort of hall I have here: reminding myself of Chateaubriand's fine account of his father going up and down a long room, half-lighted, in the old Breton castle; coming up to the table, where the family sat, and then disappearing into the gloom; while owls hooted and dogs barked in the stormy night abroad." [9] Surely the man who wrote and felt like that might have done something immense in the world.

II

When one reflects on this matter of Fitzgerald's idleness, one is naturally tempted to consider the various careers that might easily have been open to him and his attitude towards them so far as one can discover or divine it. The army or, better still, the navy would seem to have satisfied his active instinct best. Yet the minute one thinks of it one sees how difficult it would have been to chain down his wayward spirit to formal discipline. He often alludes to his Irish descent, and certainly he had the Irish impulsiveness, however English obstinacy may have mingled with it. Yet he goes to see the Rifles drill, and thinks it a shame they are not encouraged, and his blood seems to leap at the chance of fighting for his country.[10]

Again, like so many young Englishmen, Fitzgerald might have traveled widely, have charted strange seas and courted mad adventures. There were wild countries to be explored, wild animals to be hunted. Assuredly he lacked neither the courage nor the intelligence for such activity. Yet it did not tempt him. Even in the quickest heat of youth he took little interest in travel: "I should travel like you if I had the eyes to see that you have. . . . If anything I had seen in my short travels had given me any new ideas worth having I should travel more." [11] But the mind traveled more widely and more easily: why worry the limbs? To be sure there was a strange fascination about the thought of Italy. When he writes to his friends he writes with a sigh. There were monuments of history there, there were pictures that he would give much to *have* seen. But it was very far off and very troublesome. A trip even to France or to Holland was journey enough. Since you could not go to the moon why bother to cross the channel? And he found that he had "no curiosity left for other places" and was "glad to get back to my own chair and bed after three or four days' absence." [12] When he took a brief run into Ireland he saw much that amused and interested him; but— well, it was not home, that was all: "In so far as this country is Ireland I am glad to be here; but inasmuch as it is not England I wish I were there." [13]

As to more sedentary occupations, it is easy to believe that Fitzgerald might have done well in the law, but difficult to imagine him attempting it. He had certainly the breadth of view that should belong to a judge, yet hardly the enthusiastic temper that should inspire an advocate or the plodding zeal that penetrates the mysteries of a tangled cause. The natural resource for such a man in America would have been some sort of business. But it is obvious that this was more remote from Fitzgerald than even law. He had the true aristocratic, perhaps Christian, contempt for the sordidness of money, at any rate as a life interest. "Oh! If we could be brought to open our eyes. I repent in ashes for reviling the Daddy (Wordsworth) who wrote that Sonnet against damned riches." [14] His practice justified his principle, so far at least as simple and frugal living could do it. He had a comfortable income and never lacked the necessaries of life, had enough to give and gave freely; but he never sighed for luxury or missed it. Yet one feels that if he could have once got interested in business, not as money-making but as success, he might have accomplished much. He was indifferent to profit but he did not propose to be cheated. He writes to Frederick Tennyson: "Though you have a microscopic eye for human character, you are to be diddled by any knave, or set of knaves, as you well know." [15] He himself might have been cheated through indolence but not through blindness.

The Englishman in Fitzgerald's position is apt to settle down into a homely country gentleman with his hounds, his tenants, his crops, his wine, and his after-dinner sleep. This again did not answer. Fitzgerald cared neither for hunting nor fishing. He likes a garden, likes to play in it. He has a certain interest in agriculture generally. "I walk about in the fields where the people are at work, and the more dirt accumulates on my shoes, that more I think I know." [16] But although in later years he had a small place of his own, he had not the means to establish a considerable estate nor any children to transmit it to. And a country squire seemed to him a rather narrow and contemptible being.[17]

Then there was politics. A man of his gifts would seem to drift naturally into the House of Commons and take a certain part in managing the destinies of the country. He loves England, believes in her past, at any rate, if he is sometimes sceptical about her future. "Well, say as you will, there is not, and never was, such a country as Old England—never were there such a gentry as the English. They will be the distinguishing mark and glory of England in history, as the arts were of Greece and war of Rome." [18] Yet it never seems to occur to him that the gentry of England are made up of just such as he, and that he must play his part to keep them equal to their ancestors. Or rather, yes, it does occur to him, and he acknowledges the deficiency even in criticizing the deficien-

cies of others. "I am ashamed to think how little
I understand of all these things; but have wiser
men, and men in place, understood much more?
Or, understanding, have they *done* what they
should?" [19] And no doubt a genuine modesty
holds him back. He does not realize that he might
do well if he tried, or that perhaps the best of the
doing is in the trying.

If politics were excluded from Fitzgerald's life,
it seems ludicrous indeed to suggest the church, for
so many years in England the refuge of the impecunious and the indolent. Fitzgerald in a uni-
form or in a wig and gown stretches the imagination enough. But Fitzgerald in a shovel hat or a
surplice is simply impossible. Even that he should
deliver a lay lecture seemed to him so great an
absurdity that his fooling with it rises to the height
of Lamb.[20] As for the pompous or unctuous
performance in a pulpit, it would have been as much
out of his power as gaudy trifling on the stage.
He knew a lot of parsons and respected them. But
he mocked them gently: "The son having a shovel-
hat, of course the father could not be left behind.
Shovel-hats (you know) came into use with the
gift of tongs." [21] And he compares his lot with
theirs with a certain modesty, but also with perhaps

a certain contentment: "He is now a quiet, satur-
nine parson with five children, taking a pipe to
soothe him when they bother him with their noise or
their misbehavior: and I!—as the Bishop of London said, 'By the grace of God I am what I
am.' " 22

So, with all these seducing pursuits about him,
he did nothing; smoked, and smoked, and let the
world glide along as it would. And he is perfectly
ready to admit the nonentity, as in the following
wonderful passage: "Well, I have been in my dear
old Bedfordshire ever since I saw you: lounging in
the country, lying on the banks of the Ouse, smok-
ing, eating copious teas (prefaced with beer) in the
country pot-houses, and have come mourning here:
finding an empty house when I expected a full one,
and no river Ouse, and no jolly boy to whistle the
time away with. Such are the little disasters and
miseries under which I labor: quite enough, however, to make one wish to kill oneself at times. This
all comes of having no occupation or sticking-point:
so one's thoughts go floating about in a gossamer
way. At least, this is what I hear on all
sides." 23

III

It must be understood that in spite of the abstract idleness Fitzgerald had occupations and avocations, plenty of them. Like many people who have no main object in life he was often busy from morning to night. But the occupations were not sufficient for him: they did not fill his heart and rattled about in it emptily. If only there were something big enough, immense enough, difficult enough to be really worthy of his gifts and efforts! Not that there is the slightest suggestion of egotism or self-sufficiency. On the contrary the attitude is always that of one who is not fit to do anything worth while and therefore prefers to do nothing at all. "They say it is a very bad thing to do nothing; but I am sure that is not the case with those who are born to blunder; I always find that I have to repent of what I have done, not what I have left undone." [24]

But at least he is not pleased or satisfied with idleness, does not revel in it, as some appear to do. Sometimes he mocks at it: "She makes herself tolerably happy down here; and wishes to exert herself, which is the highest wish a Fitzgerald can form." [25] Sometimes he regrets it and is almost

290

EDWARD FITZGERALD

ashamed of it. "Is all this poor occupation for a man who has a soul to account for? You think so certainly." [26] Again, "For all which idle ease I think I must be damned. I begin to have dreadful suspicions that this fruitless way of life is not looked upon with satisfaction by the open eyes above." [27] Somewhere in this vastly imperfect universe there ought to be a task austere enough to call out all the powers and all the passions of a yearning soul. But it must be a real task, not a play one: so many fritter away their powers and passions on trifles, after all: "One finds few in London *serious* men: I mean *serious* even in fun, with a true purpose and character whatsoever it may be." [28] So one shuts one's eyes and lies in the sun and does what pleasant or amusing thing comes along, and forgets.

Of all these diversions none, perhaps, is quite so diverting as books. The man does not pretend to be a persistent or systematic reader: "I live on in a very seedy way, reading occasionally in books which every one else has gone through at school; and what I do read is just in the same way as ladies work: to pass the time away." [29] In his horror of pedantry he probably exaggerated the superficiality of all this. But at any rate he read widely

and with evident delight, a delight even that is
naïve and simple in its enthusiastic appreciation of
the things that appeal to it. When he turns over
the great old Greek tragedies his eyes fill with
tears. And the reading was founded upon an
amount of scholarship much greater than he was
willing to allow himself credit for. He bewails his
inaccuracy, his insufficiency, complains that his imperfect Greek enables him only to grasp the sense
of his authors but not the finer and more delicate
shades. But he had the language instinct, still more
the human and the literary instinct, and this goes
further than grammars and dictionaries. There
are many trained Greek and Persian and Spanish
scholars who could not have reached what he did.

What is especially charming about Fitzgerald's
reading is the fine critical instinct of it. Not being
a professional *littérateur* he could afford to discard
academic standards and speak his mind. The
rhetorical classifications of the formal critics amused
and amazed him. They seemed like children quarreling over toys: "It is wonderful how Macaulay,
Hallam and Mackintosh could roar and bawl at
one another over such questions as which is the
greatest poet? which is the greatest work of that
greatest poet? etc., like boys at some debating

society." [30] Some authors, or more properly some books of some authors, he liked, re-read them, loved them, and they entered into his being. Others might be great or little but they were not for him, and he would not pretend they were. And this unfailing freshness makes all his critical *dicta* interesting, whether one agrees with him or not. I suppose hundreds of persons have tried to like Crabbe because Fitzgerald liked him, tried and succeeded but imperfectly. But they like Fitzgerald's liking because it is real and part of himself.

Books of the day he turned over and sometimes enjoyed, sometimes rejected, but always with the same intensely personal touch. Many of the contemporary authors were his friends and their works he regarded curiously, but critically also. The phenomenon of Browning, so conspicuous in the seventies, he watched with some interest and some disgust. To him Crabbe was better and more human. As for novels, he devoured them, but not indiscriminately. Miss Austen would not do. The Drake and Raleigh in him would not submit to her parlor manners. On the other hand Sir Walter —ah, Sir Walter, he never tires of him. The great stories must be read over and over, even with the aid of a bungling reader when the eyes give out.

'And a pilgrimage to Edinburgh and Abbotsford is one of the few journeys that really pays.

Yet a book should be put aside at any time for the sun and fresh air. And sun and fresh air might richly augment the charm of any book. There is that old haunting love of the sea. When you go off for a week's sailing and drifting, you put Aeschylus in your pocket, and the vast bass of ocean seems to make the great choruses echo with an added splendor. "It is wonderful how *The Sea* brought up this appetite for Greek: it likes to be called θάλασσα and πόντος better than the wretched word '*Sea*,' I am sure; and the Greeks (especially Aeschylus—after Homer) are full of sea-faring sounds and allusions. I think the murmur of the Ægean (if that is their sea) wrought itself into their language." [31]

Or you turn to the simple English countryside and the charm of it is inexhaustible. You do not want the wider picturesque: mountains, dim valleys, glaciers, or hurrying kaleidoscopic visions of change; just the sweet, quiet, common features of the daily landscape are enough. When you are in the desert of London, you long for them and their graces hover in your clinging memory as they did in Susan's when she heard the thrush singing in

Cheapside: "A cloud comes over Charlotte Street and seems as if it were sailing softly on the April wind to fall in a blessed shower upon the lilac buds and thirsty anemones somewhere in Essex; or, who knows, perhaps at Boulge." [32] But you do not need the lover's solicitation of absence. The delight of this natural magic is about you always, almost unconsciously: it never fails and never palls. You tread the same paths over and over and find, as it were, an increasing perception of their loveliness, even when it lulls you to sleep. "A little Bedfordshire—a little Northamptonshire—a little more folding of the hands—the same faces—the same fields—the same thoughts occurring at the same turns of road—this is all I have to tell of; nothing at all added— but the summer is gone. My garden is covered with yellow and brown leaves; and a man is digging up the garden beds before my window, and will plant some roots and bulbs for next year." [33] And perhaps, before you know it the ever-recurring thoughts transmute themselves into the highest poetry, in which nature and death—and life—are interfused:

"And this reviving herb whose tender green
 Fledges the river-lip on which we lean—
   Ah, lean upon it lightly! for who knows
 From what once lovely lip it springs unseen?" [34]

Art in its various forms offered another occupation; not, it may be, so constantly enchanting or consoling as nature, but in some respects more piquant and stimulating. Fitzgerald was always a lover of pictures. Color delighted him, even to the point of being fascinated with "a party-colored mop, so agreeable to my color-loving eyes that I have kept it in my sitting-room instead of giving it over to be trundled in the kitchen." [35] He adored the rich splendor of the old masters as well as the subtler hues of Sir Joshua and Gainsborough. He developed at times a little of the collector's passion, what would have seemed like a good deal of it, except that he smiled at himself all the while. He hunts as the collector does, and restrains himself with a huge effort as the collector does, and then turns and buys, always with the collector's excuse that what he buys can be sold again for more money: "Frail is human virtue. I thought I had quite got over picture-dealing, when lo! walking in Holborn this day I looked into a shop just to show the strength of my virtue, and fell. That accursed battle-piece—I have bought it—and another picture of dead chaffinches, which Mr. C. will like, it is so well done: I expect you to give high prices for these pictures—mind that." [36]

He buys them and he takes them home and cleans them according to his own ideas, daringly but tenderly: "I washed it myself very carefully with only sweet salad oil; perfectly innocuous as you may imagine; and that, with the new lining, and the varnishing, has at least made the difference between a dirty and a clean beauty." [37]   And then he enjoys them, with delicate and decided discrimination, but also with enthusiastic delight, and his comments on them have the freshness and originality that make the charm of his comments on everything: "I like pictures that are not like nature. I can have nature better than any picture by looking out of my window. Yet I respect the man who tries to paint up to the freshness of earth and sky. Constable did not wholly achieve what he tried at; and perhaps the old masters chose a soberer scale of things as more within the compass of lead paint. To paint dew with lead!" [38]

The theatre meant less to Fitzgerald than painting because, for one who liked his ease and was used to it, it was difficult to get at, costly and uncomfortable. Yet in youth he got a great deal out of it: "I love it, and reading of it, now as much as ever I cared to see it; and that was, very much indeed." [39] The recollection of Kemble and Kean and Mrs. Siddons was always delightful: he liked to think of them and talk of them. Sometimes on his rare visits to London he looked in at the productions of later days. But Irving bored him, gave him the sense of innovation for innovation's sake; and if Fitzgerald was not an extreme conservative in everything, it must at least be said that he shrank from novelty as such.

It was with music as with the theatre. Music occupied and delighted him perhaps more than painting. He played himself, even composed at odd hours, and so got that pleasure which no public performance, however admirable, can ever quite give. But in music he did not generally like the more modern any more than on the stage. Wagner did not appeal to him, he could not get himself into the mood for it any more than for Browning. One hardly likes to think what he would have said of the recent Russians. Yet perhaps they would have touched him. If they did he would have said so without the slightest regard for consistency or the academic opinion of anyone. He might even have found something good or something interesting in the hubbub of twentieth century jazz; for hear what he can find to say of the jazz of his own time: "Are you overrun in London with 'Champagne

Charlie is my Name'? A brutal thing; nearly
worthless—the tune, I mean—but yet not quite—
else it would not become so great a bore. No: I
can see, to my sorrow, that it has some go—which
Mendelssohn had not. But Mozart, Rossini, and
Händel had." [40] With Mozart and Händel,
and Greek tragedy, and the sea, and country flowers and thoughts, a man's idleness need not be
emptiness.

IV

Also, there was a world of personal relations to
engage one. Fitzgerald rarely allowed himself to
be much entangled by these; but he was no complete recluse or eremite, and all his life people were
more or less about him. From the formal relations and complications of society he decidedly
shrank. The big, busy whirl of London which so
greatly charmed Lamb, was foreign and distasteful
to this shy, retiring spirit: "In this big London,
all full of intellect and pleasure and business, I
feel pleasure in dipping down into the country, and
rubbing my hand over the cool dew upon the pas-
tures, as it were." [41] In his youth he had perhaps mingled in the throng, had perhaps laughed
and trifled and danced as they did. But as years

came upon him, it all seemed too much effort and too much trouble, and led nowhere. He sees a picture of a ball: "I think the empty faces of the dance room were never better done. It seems to me wonderful that people can endure to look on such things; but I am forty, and got out of the habit now, and certainly shall not try to get it back ever again." [42] His shyness and his silence grew upon him and his avoidance of the merely conventional meetings of men and women. The shallowness of the world wearied him and its evil thoughts and evil speech disgusted him. "I was at a party of modern wits last night that made me creep into myself, and wish myself away talking to any Suffolk old woman in her cottage, while the trees murmured without. The wickedness of London appals me; and yet I am no paragon." [43]

All the same, he loved the society of people who were cordial and familiar and worth talking to. How agreeable is his account of his visit to Miss Edgworth in Ireland, when they discussed the past and extolled Sir Walter and were "merry all the day long." [44] Or he goes to a picnic in the country with a gay, congenial company, and clearly no one enjoys the frolic more than he. "Cold veal pies, champagne, etc., make up the enchantment.

We dabbled in the water, splashed each other, forded the river, climbed the rocks, laughed, sang, eat, drank, and were roasted, and returned home, the sun sinking red." [45] It is sometimes difficult to analyze the charm of Fitzgerald's rendering of all these things; but it seems to lie in the absolutely direct, sensitive vision, combined with perfect simplicity of utterance. He conveys his own impression with a delicacy and an ease that have rarely been surpassed. Take another social picture, this time of children, whom Fitzgerald loved with a special, though perhaps remote and not very communicative tenderness: "The children here are most delightful; the best company in all the world, to my mind. If you could see the little girl dance the polka with her sisters! Not set up like an infant Terpsichore, but seriously inclined, with perfect steps in perfect time." [46] You think you are seeing a child of Sir Joshua.

And if Fitzgerald did not care to mingle socially in the world, he liked to watch it in its varied phases and manifestations. Profoundly human himself under all the shyness and quiet, the ups and downs of human life, its movements and passions and vagaries, always interested him intensely. He liked to get it out of books and blend it with the

301

surrounding sweet of nature, making a compound of strange and piquant relish. "Here is a glorious sunshiny day: all the morning I read about Nero in Tacitus, lying at full length on a bench in the garden, a nightingale singing, and some red anemones eyeing the sun manfully not far off. A funny mixture all this: Nero, and the delicacy of spring: all very human, however." [47]

Also, he liked not only to read but to go about, especially among humbler folk, and to watch their ways and chat with them. Sailors interested him, and fishermen, and farmers, and beggars, and gypsies—every simple form of humanity that did not veil its primitive instincts under fine clothes and fine manners, so called. Sometimes the comic side of these contacts strikes him, as with the crowd of tramps whom he made merry with good ale: "they went off flourishing their sticks, hoping all things, enduring all things, and singing some loose things." [48] Sometimes it is the tragedy which he depicts—and feels—with singular vividness, as in the account of the poor starved actor who was drowned on the sands and huddled with spectacular expedition past the watcher's window: "I often remember the dull trot of men up the windy street, and our running to the window, and the dead head, hair, and shoulders hurried past. That was tragedy, poor fellow, whatever parts he had played before." [49] Nor is the sympathy merely abstract or sentimental. There is never any pretence or display of philanthropy, but one feels a heart and hand always ready to relieve suffering when possible. For instance, we read of the poor lad who is brought down from a London office to get a breath of the fresh country air which he needs and loves.[50]

But Fitzgerald's sympathy and tenderness were chiefly manifested in his intercourse with his intimate friends, and there is a flavor of affection and devotion in his letters to them which is unusually and singularly winning. It is true that this was a matter of mood with him, and that in everything he indulged his moods. "Pray write when you can to me; and when my stars shine so happily about my head as they do at this minute, when my blood feels like champagne, I will answer you." [51] It is true also that he was prone to analyze friendship, as other things, and even friendship is not always proof against too much analysis. There were strange strands of question and difficulty mingled with the tenderest associations. "It may seem odd to you at first—but not

perhaps on reflection—that I feel more—nervous,
I may say—at the prospect of meeting with an old
friend, after all these years, than of any indifferent
acquaintance." [52]   Again, friendship might be
like wine, its very richness made it necessary to rest
and recover afterwards: "I do not walk with him,
as my feet have been out of order, and besides I
like a long interval of fallow, even after *his* company." [53]

Moreover, Fitzgerald's absolute frankness and
independence showed in a free—gentle and dignified—but free criticism of his friends, as of others.
Some of them were authors of distinction and
prominence, as Tennyson, Thackeray, and Carlyle.
Their work often pleased Fitzgerald and he said so.
But often it did not please him, at any rate pleased
him less, and this also he indicated clearly, sometimes to other correspondents. To conceal what he
felt was possible, though when writing to those he
loved, not always easy; to say what he did not feel
was quite out of the question. He made no attempt at it.

But, criticism or no criticism, there was no doubt
about his affection for the friends who were celebrated and for those who were not. His power of
expressing tenderness in simple, direct phrases is

peculiar, and the evident absolute sincerity makes the tenderness more marked. How often and how charmingly does he return to his love for Spedding, with touches of raillery, with good-humored, kindly fun, but so clearly with the deepest, abiding regard. How richly does old, long-cherished devotion well up in this passage referring to the death and funeral of an old friend: "I want to keep clear of Woodbridge and all friends, and to talk to nobody about one who has left nobody I care to talk to him about: except Drew; and I almost dread becoming too sad with remembering our old days." [54] And Fitzgerald's friends thoroughly reciprocated his feeling for them, as is shown by Thackeray's remark, when asked, not long before his death, whom he had loved most! "Why, dear old Fitz, to be sure."

On the other hand, in the relations of life which are conventionally supposed to imply affection, Fitzgerald sometimes appears with a coolness which is startling. He would not pretend, he could not pretend. Some of his relatives he is moderately fond of, and says so. But he is apt to speak even of the nearest with as much detachment as if they were inhabitants of Mars. This perhaps shows most in the extraordinary passage about his mother:

"My mother used to come up sometimes, and we children were not much comforted. She was a remarkable woman, as you said in a former letter; and as I constantly believe in outward beauty as an index of a beautiful soul within, I used sometimes to wonder what feature in her fine face betrayed what was not so good in her character. I think (as usual) the lips: there was a twist of mischief about them now and then, like that in—the tail of a cat! —otherwise so smooth and amiable." [55] Rather different from Cowper's verses to his mother's picture!

The same comments apply to Fitzgerald's singular marriage. There is little sign of early, passionate love with him, though very likely he went through it. But as the years flowed on, he seemed to settle down to bachelorship and to appreciate his utter unfitness for anything else: "If I were conscious of being stedfast and good humored enough, I would marry tomorrow. But a humorist is best by himself." [56] Then his Quaker friend Barton died, his daughter was left unprovided for, and Fitzgerald married her, apparently out of pure philanthropy. The result was what might have been expected. They parted, oh, decently, amiably. No doubt the husband did the considerate thing in every way. All the same, I should like to know what Mrs. Fitzgerald felt about it.

The same frankness, the same distrust of convention and prejudice that characterized Fitzgerald in ordinary personal relations appear in what should perhaps be the deepest personal relation of all, the relation to God. Religion—profound, abstract thinking of every kind—always touched him, appealed to him. He could go deep enough for it, reach high enough for it: there is no doubt about that. But he was shy of theorizing, of dogmatic and positive statements about anything. In his youth he was for a time possessed by notions of vegetarianism. Beyond that, theories of any kind do not seem to have had much hold upon him. He avowed no creeds, paraded no final conclusions: others might think they saw their way, he did not.

Yet there was nothing of aggressive agnosticism in this attitude, of assertion that because he did not know, no one could. On the contrary there was humility and simplicity, a vast sense of involving ignorance, of a veil of mystery which his vision, at least, was not keen enough to penetrate. "I don't know any one who has thought out any thing so little as I have. I don't see to any end, and should keep silent till I have got a little more, and that

307

little better arranged." [57] It was his tone through life.

Such scepticism may have its evils: it blights action and fosters idleness. But it has advantages also. It carries with it, for one thing, independence, and Fitzgerald's thinking was as independent in philosophy as it was in literature or art. He would not get involved in systems. "Nothing is more wonderful to me than seeing such men as Spedding, Carlyle, and I suppose Froude, straining fact to theory as they do, while a scatter-headed Paddy like myself can keep clear." [58] Also there is tolerance, the feeling that others may be right even if you do not see it. And in Fitzgerald's case this tolerance went further to a keen sympathy with every form of simple and sincere spiritual ardor. How impressive is his account of a Bedford revival: "Oh this wonderful wonderful world, and we who stand in the middle of it are all in a maze, except poor Matthews of Bedford, who fixes his eyes upon a wooden cross and has no misgiving whatsoever. When I was at his chapel on Good Friday, he called at the end of his grand sermon on some of the people to say merely this, that they believed Christ had redeemed them; and first one got up and in sobs declared she believed it; and then another, and then another—I was quite overset:—all poor people: how much richer than all who fill the London churches. Theirs is the Kingdom of Heaven." [59]

The most natural reflection of all this spiritual attitude is, of course, to be found in Fitzgerald's writing, and on the whole it must be said that literary labor came nearer to being a serious pursuit for him than anything else. Even here he took his own work lightly and in his modest self-depreciation refused to regard it as of any general importance. "Now I am glad to see any man do anything well; and I know that it is my vocation to stand and wait, and know within myself it *is* done well." [60] Moreover, with the exception of a few delicate pieces of prose his writing was verse translation, and no one understood better than he what an ungrateful, unworthy business translation is, as ordinarily practiced. But he did not practice it in the ordinary fashion. He took the substance of his author and remoulded it, transmuted it by the subtle alchemy of his own spirit till he produced a work of genius, perhaps different from the original but often equaling it and sometimes surpassing it. To achieve this result he labored, and labored hard. The comparison of the various revisions of the

"Omar Khayyám" abundantly proves this, and we have his own words in further testimony: "I suppose very few people have ever taken such pains in translation as I have; though certainly not to be literal. But at all cost, a thing must *live;* with a transfusion of one's own worse life if one can't retain the original's better." [61] Whatever he touched did live, and with his own life.

As to the future fate of the things, he did not much trouble himself. Anonymous publication was all he cared to attempt. Not that he did not know well enough what fame was: "I was sitting at breakfast alone, and reading some of Moore's songs, and thinking to myself how it was fame enough to have written but one song—air, or words —which should in after days solace the sailor at the wheel, or the soldier in foreign places! to be taken up into the life of England!" [62] But it hardly occurred to him that any such glory might fall to him. What he did he did perfectly because his own instinct was for perfection. Whether others cared was their concern, not his. As to the immense appreciation that has fallen to his letters, he certainly never dreamed of it when writing them or at least he would have taken the pains to give them dates.

310

Yet he wrote a poem which to some of us seems, with the elegies of Matthew Arnold, to be the most substantial relic that has come from the Victorian age. The "Omar Khayyám" is too deep and has too many shadows ever to have the public-school popularity of Gray, any more than Leopardi could have it. But for those who feel its music and its melancholy few poems have a stronger hold upon the heart. Take the extraordinary invention of the stanza alone, the rhymeless third line intruding its persistent question between the recurrence of the other three, as if suggesting that the eternal order of the universe would yield a deadly monotony if it were not perpetually broken by a vague and inexplicable dissonance. Above all, the poem is interesting to us because it affords an epitome of Fitzgerald's life; that earnest, questing idleness, that haunting sense of power wasted because there is nothing in infinity adequate to employ it.

"We are no other than a moving row
    Of magic shadow-shapes that come and go
        Round with the sun-illumin'd lantern held
    In midnight by the Master of the Show." [63]

Or again the doubt is flashed forth with sharp, subtle intensity and brevity:

311

"Oh, Thou who man of baser clay didst make,
  And even with Paradise devise the Snake:
    For all the sin wherewith the face of Man
  Is blacken'd—Man's forgiveness give—and take!" [64]

But there is another passage of Fitzgerald's
translation, less known than the "Omar" yet even
more expressive of the finer and nobler side of his
character and thought; that is the conclusion of
Calderon's "Life a Dream" or, as Fitzgerald characteristically renders it, "Such Stuff as Dreams are
Made of." In these lines the substance of the
thought is as much above the original as the solemn
splendor of the iambics is above the agile ease of
the Spanish verses:

                              "Such a doubt
  Confounds and clouds our mortal life about.
  And, whether wake or dreaming, this I know,
  How dreamwise human glories come and go;
  Whose momentary tenure not to break,
  Walking as one who knows he soon may wake,
  So fairly carry the full cup, so well
  Disordered insolence and passion quell,
  That there be nothing after to upbraid
  Dreamer or doer in the part he played,
  Whether tomorrow's dawn shall break the spell,
  Or the last trumpet of the eternal day,
  When dreaming with the night shall pass away."

NOTES

II. VOLTAIRE

Unless otherwise specified, the references are to the eighteen volumes of the *Correspondance de Voltaire,* forming volumes thirty-three to fifty of *Œuvres Complètes de Voltaire,* edition 1880.

1. To Madame du Deffand, June 1, 1770, *Correspondance,* vol. xv, p. 93.
2. To Condorcet, February 6, 1775, *Correspondance,* vol. xvii, p. 221.
3. *Nouveaux Lundis,* vol. xii, p. 110.
4. *Les Contemplations,* Quelque Mots à un Autre.
5. To Thieriot, December 26, 1760, *Correspondance,* vol. ix, p. 126.
6. To D'Argental, May 21, 1761, *Correspondance,* vol. ix, p. 301.
7. To D'Olivet, September 19, 1761, *Correspondance,* vol. ix, p. 448.
8. To Devaux, October 26, 1761, *Correspondance,* vol. ix, p. 498.
9. To Frederick the Great, February 23, 1740, *Correspondance,* vol. iii, p. 386.
10. To D'Argental, June 20, 1774, *Correspondance,* vol. xvii, p. 20.
11. To D'Argental, September 23, 1750, *Correspondance,* vol. v, p. 181.
12. To Beaumont, June 7, 1771, *Correspondance,* vol. xv, p. 446.

13. To Madame de Champbonin, 1739, *Correspondance*, vol. iii, p. 334.

14. To Cideville, September, 1733, *Correspondance*, vol. i, p. 383.

15. Brosses to Voltaire, October, 1761, *Correspondance*, vol. ix, p. 502.

16. *Ibid.*

17. To Madame du Deffand, January 15, 1761, *Correspondance*, vol. ix, p. 152.

18. To Chenevières, October 10, 1761, *Correspondance*, vol. ix, p. 476.

19. To Madame du Deffand, July 28, 1774, *Correspondance*, vol. xvii, p. 41.

20. To Madame du Deffand, March 21, 1764, *Correspondance*, vol. xi, p. 168.

21. To Madame de Mimeure, 1719, *Correspondance*, vol. i, p. 51.

22. To D'Argental, September 23, 1749, *Correspondance*, vol. v, p. 66.

23. To D'Argental, June 26, 1761, *Correspondance*, vol. ix, p. 342.

24. To the Duchess of Saxe-Gotha, March 25, 1761, *Correspondance*, vol. ix, p. 242.

25. To Capacelli, December 23, 1760, *Correspondance*, vol. ix, p. 121.

26. To D'Olivet, April 25, 1764, *Correspondance*, vol. xi, p. 194.

27. To D'Argental, October 15, 1750, *Correspondance*, vol. v, p. 187.

28. To Madame Denis, November 6, 1750, *Correspondance*, vol. v, p. 194.

29. To Darget, 1751, *Correspondance*, vol. v, p. 253.

30. To Helvétius, February 25, 1739, *Correspondance*, vol. iii, p. 188.

31. To Bourgelat, March 18, 1775, *Correspondance,* vol. xvii, p. 247.

32. To D'Argental, March 18, 1775, *Correspondance,* vol. xvii, p. 249.

33. To Caylus, 1739, *Correspondance,* vol. iii, p. 107.

34. To Madame Denis, August 22, 1750, *Correspondance,* vol. v, p. 158.

35. To Cardinal de Bernis, January 6, 1664, *Correspondance,* vol. xi, p. 74.

36. To D'Argental, August 9, 1761, *Correspondance,* vol. ix, p. 390.

37. To Madame de Lutzelbourg, June 8, 1764, *Correspondance,* vol. xi, p. 237.

38. To Madame du Deffand, August 8, 1770, *Correspondance,* vol. xv, p. 166.

39. To Courtivron, October 12, 1775, *Correspondance,* vol. xvii, p. 405.

40. To Thieriot, May 7, 1739, *Correspondance,* vol. iii, p. 271.

41. To M.——, March 13, 1739, *Correspondance,* vol. iii, p. 219.

42. To D'Argens, June 21, 1739, *Correspondance,* vol. iii, p. 288.

43. To D'Argental, October 4, 1760, *Correspondance,* vol. ix. p. 8.

44. To Saurin, February 28, 1764, *Correspondance,* vol. xi, p. 141.

45. To Père Bettinelli, March, 1761, *Correspondance,* vol. ix, p. 252.

46. To D'Argental, June 22, 1764, *Correspondance,* vol. xi, p. 249.

47. To Frédéric-Guillaume, November 28, 1770, *Correspondance,* vol. xv, p. 265.

48. To Colini, March 28, 1764, *Correspondance,* vol. xi, p. 171.

49. To Madame du Deffand, September 21, 1764, *Correspondance,* vol. xi, p. 323.

50. To Formont, April 1, 1740, *Correspondance,* vol. iii, p. 409.

51. To Fyot de La Marche, October 20, 1761, *Correspondance,* vol. ix, p. 483.

52. To Helvétius, February 25, 1739, *Correspondance,* vol. iii, p. 187.

53. To D'Alembert, August 31, 1761, *Correspondance,* vol. ix, p. 428.

54. To Formont, September, 1732, *Correspondance,* vol. i, p. 292.

55. To D'Argental, July 22, 1752, *Correspondance,* vol. v, p. 450.

56. Act, v, scene 2.

57. To D'Argental, March 11, 1764, *Correspondance,* vol. xi, p. 155.

58. To D'Argental, September 1, 1752, *Correspondance,* vol. v, p. 477.

59. To Cardinal de Bernis, December 28, 1761, *Correspondance,* vol. ix, p. 569.

III.   THOMAS GRAY

Unless otherwise specified, the references are to *The Letters of Thomas Gray,* edited by Duncan C. Tovey, three volumes.

1. To Wharton, March 12, 1740, *Letters,* vol. i, p. 52.

2. To Chute and Horace Mann, July, 1742, *Letters,* vol. i, p. 112.

3. To Mason, January 22, 1761, *Letters,* vol. ii, p. 197.

4. To Wharton, February 21, 1758, *Letters,* vol. ii, p. 23.

NOTES

5. To Palgrave, September 6, 1758, *Letters,* vol. ii, p. 50.
6. To Brown, 1764, *Letters,* vol. iii, p. 41.
7. To Wharton, August 24, 1770, *Letters,* vol. iii, p. 290.
8. To Mason, 1765, *Letters,* vol. iii, p. 96.
9. To Walpole, January 12, 1735, *The Letters of Gray, Walpole, West, and Ashton* (edition Paget Toynbee), vol. i, p. 20.
10. To Walpole, March 20, 1738, *Id.,* vol. i, p. 183.
11. To Wharton, September 11, 1746, *Letters,* vol. i, p. 137.
12. To Mason, April 23, 1757, *Letters,* vol. i, p. 330.
13. To West, April 12, 1739, *Letters,* vol. i, p. 23.
14. To Mason, July 23, 1759, *Letters,* vol. ii, p. 91.
15. To Clarke, August 12, 1760, *Letters,* vol. ii, p. 166.
16. *Ibid.*
17. To Wharton, December 11, 1746, *Letters,* vol. i, p. 150.
18. To Nicholls, October, 1766, *Letters,* vol. iii, p. 124.
19. To Montagu, September 3, 1748, *Letters* (edition Toynbee), vol. ii, p. 339.
20. To his mother, June 21, 1739, *Letters,* vol. i, p. 31.
21. To Wharton, August 31, 1758, *Letters,* vol. ii, p. 47.
22. To Wharton, March 9, 1755, *Letters,* vol. i, p. 261.
23. To Clarke, August 12, 1760, *Letters,* vol. ii, p. 165.
24. To Wharton, August 5, 1763, *Letters,* vol. iii, p. 17.
25. August 26, 1766, *Letters,* vol. iii, p. 109.
26. To Mason, 1765, *Letters,* vol. iii, p. 68.
27. To Wharton, July 10, 1764, *Letters,* vol. iii, p. 36.
28. To Bonstetten, May 9, 1770, *Letters,* vol. iii, p. 282.
29. 1763, *Letters,* vol. iii, p. 14.
30. To Wharton, July 21, 1759, *Letters,* vol. ii, p. 85.
31. *Ibid.*
32. To Nicholls, June 24, 1769, *Letters,* vol. iii, p. 225.
33. To West, November 16, 1739, *Letters,* vol. i, p. 44.
34. *Childe Harold,* canto iii, stanza 72.
35. To West, December, 1736, *Letters,* vol. i, p. 3.

36. To West, April 21, 1741, *Letters,* vol. i, p. 86.
37. To Walpole, December 13, 1765, *Letters,* vol. iii, p. 98.
38. *Reminiscences,* in Tovey, *Letters,* vol. ii, p. 284.
39. To Wharton, December, 1752?, *Letters,* vol. i, p. 226.
40. To Wharton, April 26, 1744, *Letters,* vol. i, p. 119.
41. To Walpole, 1760, *Letters,* vol. ii, p. 187.
42. To Wharton, August 5, 1763, *Letters,* vol. iii, p. 17.
43. To Wharton, March 9, 1749, *Letters,* vol. i, p. 196.
44. To West, 1742, *Letters,* vol. i, p. 97.
45. To West, April, 1742, *Letters,* vol. i, p. 100.
46. To Hurd, August 25, 1757, *Letters,* vol. i, p. 347.
47. To Wharton, June 18, 1758, *Letters,* vol. ii, p. 31.
48. To Chute, 1762, *Letters,* vol. ii, p. 262.
49. To Hurd, August 25, 1757, *Letters,* vol. i, p. 346.
50. To Mason, 1757, *Letters,* vol. i, p. 350.
51. To Algarotti, September 9, 1763, *Letters,* vol. iii, p. 25.
52. To Mason, December 19, 1756, *Letters,* vol. i, p. 312.
53. To Mason, June 20, 1758, *Letters,* vol. ii, p. 34.
54. To West, August 22, 1737, *The Letters of Gray, Walpole, West and Ashton* (edition Paget Toynbee), vol. i, p. 154.
55. To Bonstetten, May 9, 1770, *Letters,* vol. iii, p. 282.
56. *Essay on Gray.*
57. To Wharton, August 21, 1755, *Letters,* vol. i, p. 272.
58. To Mason, August 1, 1757, *Letters,* vol. i, p. 343.
59. To Mason, September 21, 1753, *Letters,* vol. i, p. 237.
60. *Letters,* vol. i, pp. 291, 293.
61. To Mason, December 1, 1759, *Letters,* vol. ii, p. 115.
62. To Mason, January 3, 1758, *Letters,* vol. ii, p. 2.

IV. HORACE WALPOLE

Unless otherwise specified, the references are to *The Letters of Horace Walpole,* edited by Mrs. Paget Toynbee, sixteen volumes, with two supplementary volumes, and to *Lettres de la Marquise du Deffand à Horace Walpole,* edited by Mrs. Paget Toynbee, three volumes.

1. To Mann, April 1, 1751, *Letters,* vol. iii, p. 44.
2. To Mann, February 25, 1782, *Letters,* vol. xii, p. 182.
3. To Mann, August 17, 1749, *Letters,* vol. ii, p. 405.
4. To Mann, March 13, 1783, *Letters,* vol. xii, p. 420.
5. To the Countess of Upper Ossory, December 9, 1790, *Letters,* vol. xiv, p. 332.
6. To Mann, October 28, 1752, *Letters,* vol. iii, p. 126.
7. To Montagu, November 13, 1760, *Letters,* vol. iv, p. 457.
8. To Mann, March 11, 1750, *Letters,* vol. ii, p. 435.
9. To Mann, May 7, 1760, *Letters,* vol. iv, p. 387.
10. To Mason, February 7, 1782, *Letters,* vol. xii, p. 159.
11. To Mann, November 24, 1747, *Letters,* vol. ii, p. 295.
12. To Bentley, May 18, 1754, *Letters,* vol. iii, p. 232.
13. To Mason, April 17, 1774, *Letters,* vol. viii, p. 448.
14. To Chute, May 21, 1754, *Letters,* vol. iii, p. 237.
15. To the Countess of Upper Ossory, June 28, 1782, *Letters,* vol. xii, p. 272.
16. To Bentley, March 6, 1755, *Letters,* vol. iii, p. 291.
17. To Hannah More, July, 1788, *Letters,* vol. xiv, p. 56.
18. To Montagu, May 2, 1736, *Letters,* vol. i, p. 11.
19. To Mann, July 14, 1742, *Letters,* vol. i, p. 256.
20. To Conway, February 12, 1756, *Letters,* vol. iii, p. 398.
21. To Mann, April 14, 1743, *Letters,* vol. i, p. 340.
22. To Mann, February 12, 1772, *Letters,* vol. viii, p. 150.
23. To Bentley, May 6, 1755, *Letters,* vol. iii, p. 306.
24. To Zouch, December 9, 1758, *Letters,* vol. iv, p. 220.
25. To Mason, June 25, 1782, *Letters,* vol. xii, p. 274.
26. April 6, 1769, *Letters, Supplement,* vol. i, p. 178.
27. To Mann, March 5, 1772, *Letters,* vol. viii, p. 153.
28. To Chute, August 20, 1743, *Letters,* vol. i, p. 373.
29. To Mann, October 23, 1782, *Letters,* vol. xii, p. 350.

30. To Mary Berry, February 28, 1791, *Letters,* vol. xiv, p. 382.

31. To Chute, May 21, 1754, *Letters,* vol. iii, p. 237.

32. To Mann, February 17, 1773, *Letters,* vol. viii, p. 241.

33. To Mann, March 29, 1745, *Letters,* vol. ii, p. 79.

34. To Conway, July 20, 1744, *Letters,* vol. ii, p. 38.

35. To Conway, 1741, *Letters,* vol. i, p. 132.

36. To Mann, December 26, 1743, *Letters,* vol. i, p. 400.

37. To Walpole, December 20, 1769, *Lettres,* vol. ii, p. 38.

38. To Walpole, April 30, 1775, *Lettres,* vol. iii, p. 91.

39. To Walpole, August 6, 1779, *Lettres,* vol. iii, p. 542.

40. To Walpole, February 21, 1772, *Lettres,* vol. ii, p. 354.

41. To Walpole, May 17, 1775, *Lettres,* vol. iii, p. 96.

42. To Walpole, October 3, 1773, *Lettres,* vol. ii, p. 536.

43. To Walpole, January 3, 1776, *Lettres,* vol. iii, p. 156.

44. To Walpole, November 27, 1771, *Lettres,* vol. ii, p. 312.

45. To Walpole, July 22, 1778, *Lettres,* vol. iii, p. 447.

46. To Walpole, October 15, 1769, *Lettres,* vol. ii, p. 4.

47. To Walpole, October 9, 1770, *Lettres,* vol. ii, p. 172.

48. To Walpole, July 8, 1772, *Lettres,* vol. ii, p. 419.

49. To Walpole, August 27, 1780, *Lettres,* vol. iii, p. 614.

50. To Mary Berry, May 12, 1791, *Letters,* vol. xiv, p. 429.

51. To Mary Berry, October 10, 1790, *Letters,* vol. xiv, p. 295.

52. To Mary Berry, July 31, 1789, *Letters,* vol. xiv, p. 174.

V. WILLIAM COWPER

Unless otherwise specified, the references are to *The Correspondence of William Cowper,* edited by Thomas Wright, four volumes.

1. *Memoir of the Early Life of William Cowper,* first American edition, p. 14.

2. *Memoir,* p. 15.

NOTES

3. To Newton, July 12, 1780, *Correspondence*, vol. i, p. 215.

4. To Unwin, May 27, 1782, *Correspondence*, vol. i, p. 481.

5. To Mrs. King, August 4, 1791, *Correspondence*, vol. iv, p. 104.

6. To Newton, August 11, 1790, *Correspondence*, vol. iii, p. 480.

7. To Mrs. Newton, March 4, 1780, *Correspondence*, vol. i, p. 175.

8. *Poems*, Globe edition, p. xxv.

9. *Life of Cowper*, by Thomas Wright, p. 106.

10. *Life of Cowper*, by Thomas Wright, p. 206.

11. To Teedon, February 2, 1793, *Correspondence*, vol. iv, p. 365.

12. *Life of Cowper*, by Thomas Wright, p. 40.

13. To Lady Hesketh, August 27, 1795, *Correspondence*, vol. iv, p. 490.

14. *Memoir of the Early Life of William Cowper*, p. 116.

15. To Major Cowper, October 18, 1765, *Correspondence*, vol. i, p. 52.

16. To Unwin, May 8, 1780, *Correspondence*, vol. i, p. 188.

17. *Memoir of the Early Life of William Cowper*, p. 120.

18. To "Toby," 1754, *Correspondence*, vol. i, p. 8.

19. To Rose, August 22, 1793, *Correspondence*, vol. iv, p. 439.

20. To Lady Hesketh, March 3, 1788, *Correspondence*, vol. iii, p. 239.

21. To Newton, May 3, 1780, *Correspondence*, vol. i, p. 185.

22. *Ibid.*

23. To Lady Hesketh, September 9, 1792, *Correspondence*, vol. iv, p. 287.

24. To Lady Hesketh, September 13, 1788, *Correspondence*, vol. iii, p. 316.

25. *Poems*, Globe edition, p. 289.

26. *Poems,* Globe edition, p. 191.
27. To Newton, September 18, 1784, *Correspondence,* vol. ii, p. 243.
28. *Life of Cowper,* by Thomas Wright, p. 110.
29. To Bull, June 3, 1783, *Correspondence,* vol. ii, p. 72.
30. To Newton, March 11, 1784, *Correspondence,* vol. ii, p. 173.
31. To Newton, January 26, 1783, *Correspondence,* vol. ii, p. 40.
32. To Newton, March 18, 1792, *Correspondence,* vol. iv, p. 169.
33. To Newton, March 29, 1784, *Correspondence,* vol. ii, p. 183.
34. To Lady Hesketh, December 11, 1786, *Correspondence,* vol. iii, p. 121.
35. To John Johnson, September 29, 1793, *Correspondence,* vol. iv, p. 455.
36. To Bagot, August 2, 1791, *Correspondence,* vol. iv, p. 103.
37. To John Johnson, March 23, 1790, *Correspondence,* vol. iii, p. 450.
38. *Poems,* Globe edition, p. 289.

> No noise is here, or none that hinders thought.
> .   .   .   .
> Stillness, accompanied with sounds so soft,
> Charms more than silence.

39. September 18, 1784, *Correspondence,* vol. ii, p. 244.
40. To Newton, September 9, 1781, *Correspondence,* vol. i, p. 352.
41. To Unwin, November 26, 1781, *Correspondence,* vol. i, p. 390.
42. To Hill, November 3, 1783, *Correspondence,* vol. ii, p. 127.

43. To Newton, February 16, 1782, *Correspondence,* vol. i, p. 445.

44. To Unwin, November 18, 1782, *Correspondence,* vol. ii, p. 27.

45. To Hurdis, August 9, 1791, *Correspondence,* vol. iv, p. 106.

46. To Bull, June, 1782, *Correspondence,* vol. i, p. 486.

47. To Newton, September 18, 1781, *Correspondence,* vol. i, p. 356.

48. To Lady Hesketh, December 8, 1798, *Correspondence,* vol. iv, p. 505.

49. To Newton, April 22, 1785, *Correspondence,* vol. ii, p. 314.

50. To Unwin, April 1, 1782, *Correspondence,* vol. i, p. 470.

51. To Lady Hesketh, May 15, 1786, *Correspondence,* vol. iii, p. 36.

52. To Newton, January 13, 1787, *Correspondence,* vol. iii, p. 140.

53. To Newton, March 18, 1792, *Correspondence,* vol. iv, p. 167.

54. See the elaborate study of Cowper in *Causeries du Lundi,* vol. xi.

55. To Lady Hesketh, May 15, 1786, Correspondence, vol. iii, p. 34.

56. To Hill, November, 1784, *Correspondence,* vol. ii, p. 267.

57. To Hurdis, June 13, 1791, *Correspondence,* vol. iv, p. 75.

58. *Life of Cowper,* by Thomas Wright, p. 349.

59. To Unwin, March 18, 1782, *Correspondence,* vol. i, p. 466.

60. To Hayley, July 7, 1793, *Correspondence,* vol. iv, p. 422.

VI. CHARLES LAMB

Unless otherwise specified, the references are to *The Letters of Charles Lamb*, edited by Alfred Ainger, two volumes.

1. To Southey, August 9, 1815, *Letters*, vol. i, p. 293.
2. To Coleridge, May 27, 1796, *Letters*, vol. i, p. 2.
3. To Coleridge, June, 1796, *Letters*, vol. i, p. 15.
4. To Manning, March 1, 1800, *Letters*, vol. i, p. 114.
5. To Manning, January 2, 1810, *Letters*, vol. i, p. 256.
6. To Manning, January 2, 1810, *Letters*, vol. i, p. 257.
7. To Chambers, 1818, *Letters*, vol. ii, p. 18.
8. Essay, *Detached Thoughts on Books and Reading*.
9. To Coleridge, October 11, 1802, *Letters*, vol. i, p. 188.
10. To Chambers, 1818, *Letters*, vol. ii, p. 18.
11. Fitzgerald to Norton, June 10, 1876, *Letters of Edward Fitzgerald* (edition Wright), vol. ii, p. 198.
12. To Godwin, September 9, 1801, *Letters*, vol. i, p. 176.
13. To Mrs. Shelley, July 26, 1827, *Letters*, vol. ii, p. 170.
14. To Godwin, November 10, 1803, *Letters*, vol. i, p. 208.
15. *Ibid.*
16. To Barton, March 20, 1826, *Letters*, vol. ii, p. 143.
17. To Payne, 1823, *Letters*, vol. ii, p. 72.
18. To Payne, 1823, *Letters*, vol. ii, p. 73.
19. To Manning, February 26, 1808, *Letters*, vol. i, p. 245.
20. To Coleridge, October 23, 1802, *Letters*, vol. i, p. 190.
21. To Wordsworth, October 13, 1800, *Letters*, vol. i, p. 142.
22. To Mrs. Montagu, 1828, *Letters*, vol. ii, p. 202.
23. *The Works of Charles Lamb*, edited by Thomas Noon Talfourd (American edition), vol. ii, p. 413.
24. To Miss Betham, June 1, 1816, *Letters*, vol. i, p. 307.
25. To Chambers, 1818, *Letters*, vol. ii, p. 19.
26. To Wordsworth, March 20, 1822, *Letters*, vol. ii, p. 39.
27. To Dodwell, July, 1816, *Letters*, vol. i, p. 309.

28. To Barton, July 25, 1829, *Letters,* vol. ii, p. 230.
29. April 10, 1829, *Letters,* vol. ii, p. 223.
30. To Manning, November 3, 1800, *Letters,* vol. i, p. 146.
31. To Manning, February, 1803, *Letters,* vol. i, p. 197.
32. Essay, *A Chapter on Ears.*
33. To Hood, September 18, 1827, *Letters,* vol. ii, p. 178.
34. To Southey, October 26, 1818, *Letters,* vol. ii, p. 16.
35. To Barton, July 10, 1823, *Letters,* vol. ii, p. 81.
36. To Manning, November, 1802, *Letters,* vol. i, p. 193.
37. January 30, 1801, *Letters,* vol. i, p. 165.
38. *Ibid.*
39. *Ibid.*
40. To Coleridge, June 10, 1796, *Letters,* vol. i, p. 13.
41. To Wordsworth, August 9, 1815, *Letters,* vol. i, p. 295.
42. *Memoirs, Journal, and Correspondence of Thomas Moore,* vol. iii, p. 136.
43. Essay, *Imperfect Sympathies.*
44. To Coleridge, 1800, *Letters,* vol. i, p. 160.
45. To Mrs. Wordsworth, February 18, 1818, *Letters,* vol. ii, p. 11.
46. To Coleridge, March 9, 1822, *Letters,* vol. ii, p. 37.
47. To Dibdin, June, 1826, *Letters,* vol. ii, p. 150.
48. To Rickman, April 10, 1802, *Letters,* vol. i, p. 180.
49. *The Works of Charles Lamb* (edition Talfourd), vol. ii, p. 78.
50. To Manning, March, 1803, *Letters,* vol. i, p. 198.
51. To Coleridge, December 10, 1796, *Letters,* vol. i, p. 53.
52. To Wordsworth, April 26, 1816, *Letters,* vol. i, p. 305.
53. To Manning, February 26, 1808, *Letters,* vol. i, p. 247.
54. To Coleridge, October 9, 1800, *Letters,* vol. i, p. 141.
55. *Letters,* vol. i, p. 123.
56. To Procter, April 13, 1823, *Letters,* vol. ii, p. 75.
57. To Coleridge, November 14, 1796, *Letters,* vol. i, p. 47.
58. To Robinson, January 20, 1827, *Letters,* vol. ii, p. 158.

59. To Coleridge, May 12, 1800, *Letters,* vol. i, p. 117.
60. To Miss Wordsworth, June 14, 1805, *Letters,* vol. i, p. 213.
61. *Ibid.*
62. Fitzgerald to Norton, June 10, 1876, *Letters of Edward Fitzgerald* (edition Wright), vol. ii, p. 198.
63. Fitzgerald to Norton, April 4, 1878, as above, vol. ii, p. 243.

VII. JOHN KEATS

Unless otherwise specified, the references are to *Letters of John Keats to his Family and Friends,* edited by Sidney Colvin.

1. To Bailey, November 22, 1817, *Letters,* p. 43.
2. *Hyperion,* Book II.
3. To Reynolds, September 21, 1817, *Letters,* p. 28.
4. To George and Thomas Keats, January 5, 1818, *Letters,* p. 52.
5. To George and Georgiana Keats, February 18, 1819, *Letters,* p. 223.
6. To George and Georgiana Keats, February 18, 1819, *Letters,* p. 222.
7. To George and Georgiana Keats, April 16, 1819, *Letters,* p. 245.
8. To Fanny Keats, August 23, 1820, *Letters,* p. 369.
9. To Reynolds, August 25, 1819, *Letters,* p. 283.
10. *Letters of John Keats to Fanny Brawne,* edited by Forman, August 17, 1819, p. 26.
11. To Haydon, April 13, 1819, *Letters,* p. 267.
12. To Taylor and Hessey, July 8, 1817, *Letters,* p. 19.
13. To George and Georgiana Keats, April 16, 1819, *Letters,* p. 245.
14. To George and Georgiana Keats, October 25, 1818, *Letters,* p. 181.

15. To George and Thomas Keats, January 23, 1818, *Letters,* p. 59.

16. To George and Georgiana Keats, April 15, 1819, *Letters,* p. 244.

17. To Georgiana Keats, January 15, 1820, *Letters,* p. 342.

18. To Reynolds, May 3, 1818, *Letters,* p. 106.

19. To Taylor and Hessey, May 16, 1817, *Letters,* p. 17.

20. To George and Georgiana Keats, March 19, 1819, *Letters,* p. 235.

21. To Bailey, November 22, 1817, *Letters,* p. 42.

22. *Ode to a Grecian Urn.*

23. To Reynolds, March 14, 1818, *Letters,* p. 83.

24. To Reynolds, February 19, 1818, *Letters,* p. 73.

25. To Jane Reynolds, September 14, 1817, *Letters,* p. 25.

26. *Hyperion,* Book I.

27. To Bailey, November 22, 1817, *Letters,* p. 43.

28. To Reynolds, April 17, 1818, *Letters,* p. 9.

29. To Reynolds, February 19, 1818, *Letters,* p. 74.

30. *Sonnet Written on a Summer Evening.*

31. To George and Georgiana Keats, September 24, 1819, *Letters,* p. 314.

32. To Bailey, March 13, 1818, *Letters,* p. 82.

33. *Letters,* p. 184.

34. To Haydon, May 10, 1817, *Letters,* p. 13.

35. To Reynolds, April 18, 1817, *Letters,* p. 9.

36. To Woodhouse, October 27, 1818, *Letters,* p. 185.

37. To Reynolds, August 25, 1819, *Letters,* p. 282.

38. *Ode to May.*

39. *Ibid.*

40. To George and Georgiana Keats, October 14, 1818, *Letters,* p. 171.

41. To George and Georgiana Keats, March 19, 1819, *Letters,* p. 234.

42. To Hessey, October 9, 1818, *Letters,* p. 167.

43. To Shelley, August, 1820, *Letters,* p. 366.
44. To Bailey, July 18, 1818, *Letters,* p. 142.
45. To George and Georgiana Keats, October, 1818, *Letters,* p. 178.
46. To Hunt, May 10, 1817, *Letters,* p. 12.
47. To George and Georgiana Keats, September, 1819, *Letters,* p. 291.
48. To George and Georgiana Keats, October, 1818, *Letters,* p. 181.
49. To Haydon, May 11, 1817, *Letters,* p. 15.
50. To George and Georgiana Keats, April 15, 1919, *Letters,* p. 238.
51. To Bailey, June 10, 1818, *Letters,* p. 113.
52. To Brown, August, 1820, *Letters,* p. 370.
53. To Bailey, July 18, 1818, *Letters,* p. 143.
54. To George and Georgiana Keats, October, 1818, *Letters,* p. 172.
55. *Epistolae,* Lib. xx, Ep. 4.
56. To George and Georgiana Keats, October, 1818, *Letters,* p. 180.
57. *The Letters of John Keats to Fanny Brawne* (edition Forman), p. lxiii.
58. To Fanny Brawne, p. 5.
59. To Brown, November 1, 1820, *Letters,* p. 374.

VIII. GUSTAVE FLAUBERT

Unless otherwise specified, the references are to *Correspondance de Gustave Flaubert,* four volumes, and to *Correspondance entre George Sand et Gustave Flaubert.*

1. To Madame X, 1852, *Correspondance,* vol. ii, p. 115.
2. To Mademoiselle Leroyer de Chantepie, March 18, 1857, *Correspondance,* vol. iii, p. 80.
3. To Madame X., October 20, 1846, *Correspondance,* vol. i, p. 179.

NOTES

4. To Madame X., 1852, *Correspondance,* vol. ii, p. 126.

5. To Bouilhet, May 24, 1855, *Correspondance,* vol. iii, p. 14.

6. To Madame Roger des Genettes, 1872, *Correspondance,* vol. iv, p. 117.

7. To Madame X., 1853, *Correspondance,* vol. ii, p. 281.

8. To Madame X., 1853, *Correspondance,* vol. ii, p. 189.

9. To Madame X., 1852, *Correspondance,* vol. ii, p. 87.

10. To Madame X., 1853, *Correspondance,* vol. ii, p. 231.

11. To Madame X., 1853, *Correspondance,* vol. ii, p. 174.

12. To Madame X., 1853, *Correspondance,* vol. ii, p. 238.

13. To Madame X., 1853, *Correspondance,* vol. ii, p. 343.

14. To Madame X., 1852, *Correspondance,* vo. ii, p. 90.

15. To Madame X., 1852, *Correspondance,* vol. ii, p. 73.

16. To Madame X., 1853, *Correspondance,* vol. ii, p. 347.

17. To Madame X., August, 1852, *Correspondance,* vol. ii, p. 91.

18. To Madame X., 1853, *Correspondance,* vol. ii, p. 367.

19. *Correspondance Sand,* pp. 67, 69.

20. To Madame X., 1853, *Correspondance,* vol. ii, p. 232.

21. To Bouilhet, June 28, 1855, *Correspondance,* vol. iii, p. 23.

22. To Madame X., 1852, *Correspondance,* vol. ii, p. 113.

23. To Madame X., 1853, *Correspondance,* vol. ii, p. 246.

24. To Madame X., 1852, *Correspondance,* vol. ii, p. 136.

25. To Madame X., 1853, *Correspondance,* vol. ii, p. 230.

26. To Madame X., 1853, *Correspondance,* vol. ii, p. 273.

27. To Madame X., 1852, *Correspondance,* vol. ii, p. 97.

28. George Sand to Flaubert, October 26, 1872, *Correspondance Sand,* p. 336.

29. To George Sand, 1867, *Correspondance Sand,* p. 86.

30. To Mademoiselle Leroyer de Chantepie, May 18, 1857, *Correspondance,* vol. iii, p. 88.

31. To Du Camp, April, 1846, *Correspondance,* vol. i, p. 101.

32. To Madame X., August 9, 1846, *Correspondance,* vol. i, p. 119.

33. To Madame X., 1853, *Correspondance,* vol. ii, p. 197.

34. To Madame X., 1852, *Correspondance,* vol. ii, p. 120.

35. To Madame X., October 4, 1846, *Correspondance,* vol. i, p. 170.

36. To Madame X., 1852, *Correspondance,* vol. ii, p. 164.

37. To Mademoiselle Leroyer de Chantepie, May 18, 1857, *Correspondance,* vol. iii, p. 87.

38. To Bouilhet, February 10, 1851, *Correspondance,* vol. ii, p. 45.

39. To Madame X., 1853, *Correspondance,* vol. ii, p. 187.

40. To Madame X., 1853, *Correspondance,* vol. ii, p. 184.

41. To Madame X., 1853, *Correspondance,* vol. ii, p. 180.

42. To Madame X., September 28, 1846, *Correspondance,* vol. i, p. 164.

43. To Madame X., August, 1852, *Correspondance,* vol. ii, p. 96.

44. To Chevalier, April 9, 1851, *Correspondance,* vol. ii, p. 50.

45. To Madame X., August 7, 1846, *Correspondance,* vol. i, p. 114.

46. To Madame X., 1853, *Correspondance,* vol. ii, p. 297.

47. To Madame X., 1852, *Correspondance,* vol. ii, p. 133.

48. To Madame X., 1853, *Correspondance,* vol. ii, p. 225.

49. To Madame X., 1853, *Correspondance,* vol. ii, p. 351.

50. To Madame X., 1853, *Correspondance,* vol. ii, p. 353.

51. To Madame X., 1851, *Correspondance,* vol. ii, p. 62.

52. To Madame X., August 7, 1846, *Correspondance,* vol. i, p. 113.

53. To Madame X., 1851, *Correspondance,* vol. ii, p. 62.

54. To Madame X., 1853, *Correspondence,* vol. ii, p. 355.

55. To Madame X., 1854, *Correspondance,* vol. ii, p. 397.
56. *Journal des Goncourts,* April 9, 1864, vol. ii, p. 187.
57. To Madame X., October 22, 1846, *Correspondance,* vol. i, p. 180.

IX. EDWARD FITZGERALD

Unless otherwise specified, the references are to *Letters of Edward Fitzgerald,* two volumes, *More Letters of Edward Fitzgerald,* and *Letters of Edward Fitzgerald to Fanny Kemble,* all edited by William Aldis Wright.

1. To Allen, May 23, 1835, *Letters,* vol. i, p. 33.
2. To Allen, November 27, 1832, *Letters,* vol. i, p. 13.
3. To Pollock, August 14, 1839, *More Letters,* p. 6.
4. To Norton, August 5, 1881, *Letters,* vol. ii, p. 317.
5. To Cowell, January 25, 1848, *Letters,* vol. i, p. 233.
6. To Mrs. Cowell, August 21, 1860, *More Letters,* p. 53.
7. To Mrs. Allen, August 15, 1857, *Letters,* vol. i, p. 338.
8. *To Fanny Kemble,* October 24, 1876, p. 111.
9. To Frederic Tennyson, November 16, 1874, *More Letters,* p. 167.
10. To Crabbe, June 4, 1861, *Letters,* vol. ii, p. 22.
11. To Frederic Tennyson, March 21, 1841, *Letters,* vol. i, p. 81.
12. To Donne, July 18, 1863, *Letters,* vol. ii, p. 40.
13. To Barton, September 2, 1841, *Letters,* vol. i, p. 90.
14. To Barton, 1844, *Letters,* vol. i, p. 168.
15. June 19, 1849, *Letters,* vol. i, p. 245.
16. To Thompson, February 18, 1841, *Letters,* vol. i, p. 79.
17. To Pollock, January 16, 1862, *More Letters,* p. 59.
18. To Frederic Tennyson, June 7, 1840, *Letters,* vol. i, p. 68.
19. To Cowell, October 3, 1857, *Letters,* vol. i, p. 341.
20. To Barton, January, 1842, *Letters,* vol. i, p. 99.

21. To Laurence, September 28, 1842, *Letters,* vol. i, p. 138.
22. To Barton, August 29, 1847, *Letters,* vol. i, p. 222.
23. To Pollock, August 14, 1839, *More Letters,* p. 4.
24. To Thompson, Good Friday, 1863, *Letters,* vol. ii, p. 37.
25. To Allen, July 12, 1840, *Letters,* vol. i, p. 70.
26. To Allen, April 21, 1837, *Letters,* vol. i, p. 49.
27. To Barton, July 24, 1839, *Letters,* vol. i, p. 62.
28. To Frederic Tennyson, May 24, 1844, *Letters,* vol. i, p. 164.
29. To Frederic Tennyson, April 10, 1839, *Letters,* vol. i, p. 58.
30. To Norton, September 10, 1876, *Letters,* vol. ii, p. 200.
31. To Donne, October 4, 1863, *Letters,* vol. ii, p. 49.
32. To Barton, April 11, 1844, *Letters,* vol. i, p. 159.
33. To Frederic Tennyson, October 10, 1844, *Letters,* vol. i, p. 176.
34. *Rubáiyát* (edition 4), stanza xx.
35. To Crabbe, September 25, 1861, *More Letters,* p. 55.
36. To Barton, September 16, 1842, *Letters,* vol. i, p. 132.
37. To Barton, November 27, 1841, *Letters,* vol. i, p. 94.
38. To Frederic Tennyson, May 24, 1844, *Letters,* vol. i, p. 165.
39. *To Fanny Kemble,* June 4, 1876, p. 105.
40. To Pollock, November 11, 1867, *More Letters,* p. 88.
41. To Barton, February 21, 1842, *Letters,* vol. i, p. 106.
42. To Carlyle, February, 1847, *Letters,* vol. i, p. 214.
43. To Barton, May, 1845, *Letters,* vol. i, p. 192.
44. To Barton, September 2, 1841, *Letters,* vol. i, p. 89.
45. To Barton, August 17, 1843, *Letters,* vol. i, p. 143.
46. To Barton, November 27, 1844, *Letters,* vol. i, p. 179.
47. To Allen, April 28, 1839, *Letters,* vol. i, p. 60.
48. To Pollock, August 14, 1839, *More Letters,* p. 5.
49. To Mrs. Allen, October 26, 1859, *Letters,* vol. ii, p. 10.
50. To Pollock, August, 1872, *More Letters,* p. 146.

NOTES

51. To Frederic Tennyson, October, 1841, *Letters,* vol. i, p. 93.
52. To Pollock, November 17, 1871, *Letters to Fanny Kemble,* p. 7.
53. To Wright, September 4, 1879, *More Letters,* p. 224.
54. To Crabbe, September 19, 1857, *More Letters,* p. 48.
55. *To Fanny Kemble,* February 27, 1872, p. 9.
56. To Frederic Tennyson, December 8, 1844, *Letters,* vol. i, p. 185.
57. To Allen, July 4, 1835, *Letters,* vol. i, p. 37.
58. To Donne, February 15, 1867, *Letters,* vol. ii, p. 92.
59. To Barton, April 11, 1844, *Letters,* vol. i, p. 160.
60. To Cowell, January 25, 1848, *Letters,* vol. i, p. 232.
61. To Cowell, April 27, 1859, *Letters,* vol. ii, p. 5.
62. To Mrs. Cowell, February, 1851, *More Letters,* p. 27.
63. *Rubáiyát* (edition 4), stanza lxviii.
64. *Rubáiyát* (edition 4), stanza lxxxi.

INDEX

INDEX

INDEX

INDEX

338

INDEX

INDEX